SALVATION CANYON

SALVATION CANYON

A True Story
of Desert Survival in Joshua Tree

Ed Rosenthal

Cover photograph: Don Graham - inkknife_2000, licensed
under CC BY-SA 4.0 (color enhanced), taken on March 18, 2017.
Interior cover map: National Park Service, Black Rock Canyon
Station, September 30, 2010, courtesy Ed Rosenthal.

Cover design: Carrie Paterson
Book design: Jonathan Yamakami

Publisher's Cataloging-in-Publication Data

Names: Rosenthal, Ed, 1946-, author.
Title: Salvation canyon : a true story of desert survival in Joshua Tree /
by Ed Rosenthal.
Description: Los Angeles, CA: DoppelHouse Press, 2020.
Identifiers: LCCN: 2020936494 | ISBN: 9781733957977 (pbk.) |
9781733957960 (ebook)
Subjects: LCSH Rosenthal, Ed, 1946-. | Joshua Tree National Park (Calif.)
| Mojave Desert. | Desert survival--California. | Wilderness survival--
California. | Wilderness survival--Biography. | Adventure and adventurers-
-United States--Biography. | Outdoor life. | BISAC BIOGRAPHY &
AUTOBIOGRAPHY / Survival | BIOGRAPHY & AUTOBIOGRAPHY /
Adventurers & Explorers | BIOGRAPHY & AUTOBIOGRAPHY / Personal
Memoirs | BIOGRAPHY & AUTOBIOGRAPHY / Jewish
Classification: LCC GV200.5 .R66 2020 | DDC 613.6/9/092--dc23

 DoppelHouse Press | Los Angeles, California

PREFACE

TEN YEARS AGO, I survived a baffling near-death experience in the Mojave Desert. To help communicate this astounding event, I researched classics of the survival genre. The first of these was Steven Callahan's masterpiece *Adrift*, which describes his unplanned crossing of the Atlantic on a lifeboat. Afterwards, I dove into scores of memoirs. But it's Callahan's journey and these few simple words from his preface that mean the most to me:

> *I am less an individual than part of a continuum,*
> *joined to all things and driven by them more than I am*
> *in control of my own path.*

Unlike Callahan, a world-class sailor and adventurer, I was a real estate broker who took solitary hikes in the desert when I closed a big deal.

> *Let's face it. When Mr. Rosenthal was lost in*
> *the desert, the temperature was*
> *115 degrees in the shade. People die in*
> *two hours in heat like that...*

Sheriff Jeff Joling
San Bernadino County, California

MISSING PERSON

- **Edward H. Rosenthal**
- **Age 64**
- **Height 5' 5"**
- **Weight 155 lbs.**

Last seen Friday, September 24 at Black Rock Campground in Joshua Tree National Park wearing a tan shirt, tan pants, and a tan hat.

Anyone who might have seen Edward Rosenthal is asked to call the Federal Interagency Communications Center at 909-383-5668.

I.

THREE MEN HELD a massive desk just outside my office. I stepped aside as they hoisted it through the doorway, carried it to the corner, and placed its plain oak top just under the window ledge.

"Thank you." I held the front edge and leaned over the top of the five-by-eight-foot gift from my client.

The lead man gasped, "Okay," and I gave them each ten bucks. The last man pulled the yawning door closed. It was a bear of a desk — and it had been a bear of a deal to close. Don Clinton had sent his father's desk to thank me.

I pulled open the flat middle drawer and found a crinkled ad from 1932 for a meal at Clifton's Cafeteria. "Two eggs, bacon, and toast for $.05 cents, coffee included." I pulled the tarnished handle of the top drawer on the left and found an old wooden contraption with a weight and a balance for measuring, and under this, a pamphlet with a drawing of a clock and bold print across the picture that read, "The clock strikes twelve."

I'd been heading out the door and was already late,

so I shoved the pamphlet in my pocket and headed out for the press conference through the marble hallway whose mahogany moldings pointed the way to the elevator. The long corridor was strung with lamps from the 1920s, opaque deco glass in sinuous black metal frames. At the polished brass elevators, I pushed the call button.

In the lobby hung a globe etched with a deco goddess lit from within by a glowing yellow bulb. Through the etched-glass entry doors onto the street, it was a short jaunt to the corner of Fifth and Spring Streets where The Preacher stood, a black man with a bible in his right hand who held forth below the historic cornices and large glass windows. I crossed Spring Street to the Rowan Building and saw, as I did each time, the shadow of the first landlord I dealt with here in Downtown Los Angeles. The vision of him, a bedraggled man in a black raincoat, screamed, "I'm going to kill that mother fucker!"

Walking these streets, my mind was haunted by memories of people I had dealt with. But the upper levels of the street were inhabited by mythological dreams. The bas relief carved into the granite base of the Stock Exchange Building reflected my own weariness with business. Crafted eighty years earlier by radical immigrant stonemasons, the huge central panel shows a goddess of enterprise with her arms draped around Karl Marx and Vladimir Lenin. At the old Alexandria Hotel, floral moldings and hour-glass balustrades decorate the roof. Classical statues stand out from the corners of the grand old hotel as the ghost of the old hotel owner barks, "I don't need any fuckin' broker to tell me what my place is worth."

Crossing Fifth Street, I was disturbed by ghosts of County policy. A decade ago, councilwoman Jan Perry pleaded with deaf Supervisors for homeless facilities. From south and north, now the sidewalks were lined with people opening and closing their bedrolls. A scene that extended deep into the Toy District.

I stepped over a sleeping woman wrapped in a dirty blanket sprawled across the sidewalk. A bent, old man covered his mouth as he coughed and extended his other hand asking for an offering. I moved aside before a wheelchair could knock me down.

At Sixth and Spring, the scene brightened. Slim young women in skirts that floated just above the bottom of their hips blended with lost young men in stained fatigues. Swank new clubs and restaurants had recently opened inside the historic bank buildings.

A thin yellow tape on plastic orange posts diverted traffic at Broadway and Seventh Street. Across the glass front of Clifton's Cafeteria, a ceremonial ribbon had been draped awaiting the ribbon-cutting ceremony. It signaled the end of seven arduous years. I'd closed the deal.

People are not intrigued by real estate, but a large crowd had gathered, covering the sidewalk and spreading out into the street. This particular deal had captured the public's imagination. It was the well-known disposition of the founder, Clifford Clinton, who provided free meals throughout the Great Depression, and the environment he'd created, an inspiration for Disney's Disneyland, with its faux forest and cute wooden bears climbing trees and a giant redwood stump at its center.

A podium was positioned on the historic ter-razzo sidewalk. I was just in time. I elbowed my way through the crowd, circled the last of the orange posts, and closed in on the building's metal facade, where the City councilman's spokesperson had a pair of large cardboard scissors in her hand. A panhandler extended his palm: "Do you have a cigarette man?"

I wriggled sideways through a line of reporters and positioned myself a few feet in front of Jessica as the ceremony began. Don stood at the podium. "We finally found someone to carry our family legacy." The buyer stepped forward. The cafeteria workers were in a line along the curb, their ears open for news of their future.

"We will continue the legacy of Clifford Clinton," the buyer said, and the workers applauded with relief.

I stared at Jessica, who bathed everybody in congratulations, but had forgotten me.

"Our office has worked closely with the Clinton family and Andrew the preservationist to bring this to fruition and..." My glaring gaze caught her eye. "I see Ed Rosenthal is here, the Historic Properties Broker who made the deal." Mission accomplished. Don and Andrew took positions beside her, and with all their hands on the make-believe scissors, they cut the red satin ribbon.

Clogs of die-hards lingered and exchanged memories. Some recollected the cute little bears; others, Easter Sundays with pecan pie. I drew Don and Andrew to my side below the CLIFTON'S sign and had a bystander take a photo. With the phone back in my pocket, I walked away.

After seven years of deal making, I was done rolling file boxes through parking garages into elevators. We had found a buyer, and a check would be made payable to me. I took a lighthearted walk north on Broadway to Sixth Street. I wouldn't be in Downtown L.A. for at least a week. I wouldn't speak to a broker, buyer, or seller of real estate. I was on my way to the Mojave.

I got into my car at the parking lot on Sixth and Main, exited in front of the Pacific Electric Building, turned left, went north to Fifth Street, and within a few blocks was on the Harbor Freeway. My mind drifted back to my first dead-end job in Los Angeles as an overnight security guard at the chemical plant on Terminal Island.

My headlights lit the dark as I parked in the plant's empty lot. With a giant step on a concrete stair, I opened the metal door. The tiny room had a desk with a worn book wrapped in red tape. The cover read "Security Guard Manual." There was a schedule on the first page that indicated rounds every half-hour. It mapped out a series of stops along corridors with pictures of each security station, where the guard was to insert and turn a key as he made the rounds. Silver-taped pipes hung above me as I stumbled in the dark on wood planks to reach every spot to turn each key. The lumpy pipes rumbled overhead. I kept walking, hesitating at the turns as the route on each floor turned unpredictably. Sometimes the pipes above bent in a different direction or just flopped and hung in the dark. The walk along the planks on each floor corridor ended in a narrow metal stairway ascending to the next level. The floors were unevenly spaced. The higher I went, the darker it got.

The spooky memory left a smile on my face as I merged onto the 10 West. Traffic towards the desert was on the other side of the road. I'd be in my quiet, enchanted place tomorrow, but now the trunk of my car held the chaos of packing and unpacking my life over the last few years through three different firms, and it needed unloading and reorganizing. I got off the freeway near home and drove to Bed Bath & Beyond.

The felt-lined trunk had books, clothing, and hiking gear stuffed in every corner. I wanted to help it reflect my new priorities, whatever it was I finally felt free to focus on. I walked into the feminized box canyons and looked around, below and above, at the crated and loose offerings. After a few questions, I realized my needs weren't standard.

"What do you have for dividing up parts of a trunk?"

"There's some wire boxes, if you turn left by furnishings."

Those proved rigid and ugly, so I drifted on, through the corridors to the registers and special offerings in bins. A woman with a cart full of toddlers and boxes passed by. She had a cute rattan container in her loot.

"Excuse me, where did you get that rattan piece?"

She pointed over the head of one toddler to the store's rear corner near a sign that read "Returns." I wriggled through a sea of females and found them: the woven boxes with an auburn tinge and no loose ends. I saw how to use them and took one in each hand. In the busy parking lot, I opened the trunk, pushed the loose items to the back and made room for the new boxes. I placed the ten-inch rattan box on the left and the six-inch-high one adjacent so both would be right in my face when the lid swung open. I filled them with my priority items: Cliff Bars, compass, emergency lights, water purifier, and knife. With all my books in the short rattan case, I made a miniature mobile library shelf.

I called my wife. "Honey, you're right about Bed Bath & Beyond. I found the best little containers."

"Oh, that's great, when will you be home?"

"Probably by four-thirty."

"Did you check the weather report for the desert?"

"Don't worry about that. I have to pull off. Let's talk later."

She was concerned with the weather.

At our terra-cotta tiled complex, the wide wrought-iron entry swung open. After waiting for a few scream-ing kids on bicycles to move aside, I got through the gate. At our unit, I turned the car around to back into the garage and left the trunk popped open so Nicole would see the baskets when she got home. Excited to position items in my new rattan containers, I carried my empty water bottles through the laundry room and crossed the white entry tiles to the kitchen. She had prettied up the entry counter with a bouquet of plump pink and violet dahlias in a small silver vase. I filled my red and blue hiking bottles to the brim, tightened the black tops, strode back to the garage, and shoved the glistening vessels snug into my newly installed left compartment. When I saw the bottles in their new setup, it felt like my brain had been rearranged.

I headed up the beautiful hardwood stairs that led to our second story landing. An Armenian craftsman seemed to pull these perfect oak planks from his hat. My wife had access to artists and artisans. She'd grown up in Los Angeles, so she knew people like the young woman who'd painted the beautiful blue and rose canvas hanging above our couch in the living room. It matched a jade end table with flowers etched into its sides.

We'd met through a matchmaker after I'd had an epiphany while alone at LACMA one day. I was on a bench in front of a Roy Lichtenstein lithograph. I was forty and had been dating the wrong women for a long time. I wanted a child but was nowhere close to finding a wife. The Lichtenstein female seemed a caricature of the many women I'd met, with sexy red lips and overdone lashes. Her face was shocked. She held her head in her hand. The cartoon bubble read, "I can't believe it. I forgot to have children."

From the padded bench, I stared at the lithograph. Oblivious to the men and women walking in front of me, standing behind me, admiring other art in the gallery, it was as if Lichtenstein had knocked me on the head with his knuckles.

"I forgot to have children."

I enlisted a Jewish matchmaker and for fifty dollars got a great deal in meeting my wife, a kind-hearted social worker. Nicole, a lovely, petite blonde, who felt like home.

When the time came for one of my trips, I was a whistling tea kettle with my old friend Frank's happy marriage advice steaming out the top. I needed to get to as remote a place as I could, even if my wife knew where I was. The further she had reached in to get hold of my adventure, the less I liked it. After I sold the groundbreaking 2121 Lofts project, a conversion of an old industrial property into a gardenlike community, and got a huge commission, I went on a hiking trip in New Zealand. I was thumbing through magazines in the lobby when the concierge announced, "Your wife is on the phone."

"Hi, Honey, enjoying your trip?"

"Yes, it's fine."

"I tried to arrange a special massage for you but the schedule got screwed up."

"That's okay. You didn't have to do that."

"What's wrong?"

"Nothing is wrong. You know I don't like contact on my trips."

Now passing by Nicole's makeup table, I saw myself in the oval mirror above her gold and green perfume bottles and open makeup trays. The mirrored doors of my closet were open. I pulled down the soft black bag I used for my desert trips. I hardly needed anything — just some shorts and a short sleeve shirt for my day hike Friday. Then not much more than a paisley yellow and white bathing suit for laying around the pool on Saturday. With the travel bag on the satin comforter of our bed, I tossed in my white short-sleeve shirt and tan shorts. I filled the bag with three pairs of underwear, a few t-shirts, and socks. It took all of five minutes to pack.

Downstairs, the garage door opened and shut. I heard Nicole's heels click across the entry tiles. The downstairs bathroom door closed. After two minutes, I heard my wife's voice bounce off the landing and into the upstairs hall, "Hi, Honey. Getting ready for your trip?"

I walked out of our bedroom, down the corridor, past a watercolor of desert rocks. "Yeah. Did you see my new containers from Bed Bath & Beyond?"

"They look nice," she shouted up the polished wooden steps. "Honey, did you hear the weather report for the desert?" There was a measured, false lack of urgency in her voice. I disappeared into the bedroom again and waited a while, then went back on the landing. Nicole was already in the kitchen, so I projected my voice, knowing it would reach her.

"It's just my usual trip."

Her steps returned. "Maybe you should just lie around at the pool. A heat wave is scheduled to hit the desert just when you're going. This weekend."

"Don't worry, it's the same hike I always do. You have a lot planned for the weekend, right? Aren't you picking up Kathy from the airport?"

"Yeah. Are you going to the same place?"

"I am. Don't worry, it's the same place I always go."

Thursday, after a jerky night's sleep, Nicole and I went downstairs. I filled my cooler with salads, milk, and juices for the trip. I'd done this same desert escape ten to fifteen times. Aside from a three-hour hike, I'd spend most of my time lounging around the motel getting stoned, writing poetry, and reading. I rushed the cooler out to my car before we sat down for breakfast. I filled my bowl with the special granola I bought for my getaways, and Nicole handed me some milk. The grocery bag on the kitchen table bulged with bread, chips, and treats from Trader Joe's to accompany me in the passenger seat on the long ride to the desert. My wife hid behind her newspaper as I gobbled down my cereal, clutched the bag in one hand, got up, crossed the laundry room, pushed open the door to the garage, and threw this last item into the car. It was launch time for the long-anticipated break for freedom. I rushed inside to the kitchen and gave my wife a quick kiss on her forehead, careful not to interfere with her daily practice of obituary perusal. "Have a safe trip!" she turned from her pages to say.

"I'll call Sunday as usual. Anything you want me to tell Hilary?" I was meeting our daughter.

"No, don't worry." She got up and kissed me goodbye.

The garage door clanked behind me, and I began to relax. The tension below my eyes that had felt like my nose was crunched up in a frown left me now. I leaned back in the seat and let my hands relax on the steering wheel. With one last thing to do before I headed to the desert, I took the 10 Freeway west to hook up with my daughter in Santa Monica. I was an hour ahead of our meet-up time so I went into Forever Twenty-One to fulfill a longstanding father and daughter tradition.

I told the clerk, "I'd like an $18, a $36, and one $54 card." By making sure each was a multiple of the number eighteen, I threw in the extra blessings of Jewish mystical numerology. She was turning twenty-one but still felt to me like the fragile four-pound infant she had been when they finally released her from the neonatology ward.

Two months after her birth, I had carried her from our car. Nicole was in the bedroom getting the bassinet ready. The mummy-like bundle wrapped in soft white cottons sat beside me on the wide living room couch. I called out, "Nicole, what should I do with her?"

"Nothing. Wait a minute."

I looked down at the doll-like face and withered, afraid to touch her.

"Okay, bring her in."

"How should I carry her?"

"What?"

"Never mind." I held Hilary out in front of me with stiff arms, carried her into our room, then placed the delicate being into her bassinet and breathed again.

Hilary opened the door to the bagel place in Santa Monica, and I walked up to meet her. We hugged hello. Her hair was tied in a comfortable bun, and I didn't notice any new hair colorations or extra piercings.

"How is everything going?" I asked the bubbly young adult.

"Everything is very good, Dad."

"Your new place is so close to Santa Monica College; it will be easy to get to school. Have you picked out a major yet?"

"No, Dad. But probably teaching."

Grateful that Hilary had survived her birth, we had given our only child a lot of freedom. Now a grown woman, she had spent two years circling between her classes in Santa Barbara, friends in L.A., our home, and her aunt's place in Santa Ynez. I handed her the gift cards.

"Dad, that's so nice." She kissed my cheek. We walked past the sprinkle trays at the ice cream niche and then up the promenade to Forever Twenty-One.

Hilary asked the clerk, "Do you have a chair for my Dad to sit in? He always waits when I shop."

The clerk pulled out a chair from behind her counter. I visualized Friday afternoon. I saw myself approaching my car in the parking lot at the end of my glorious hike and taking a seat on the rear bumper to remove my boots, tossing them into my trunk and slipping on my loafers. I felt the drive down Route 62 to the motel. I would park and go to my room to put on my bathing suit and grab some snacks. After a few steps down to the rust pavers of the pool landing, I'd be lying back, mission accomplished, totally relaxed at a spot under the roof awning with a black shadow covering me. I'd have the *New York Times* handy and some Medjool dates in a bowl.

"I finished." My eyes opened, and I went around the counter to meet her. She had a stuffed bagful of clothes in her hand and a smile on her face.

"Everything worked out great. I have one coupon left. I'll come back with Berna next week. Look at this cute blouse." She held it against her chest.

"That's very pretty." I smiled without examining the pattern or colors of the item. I cared for the ritual. When she was little, on Sundays I'd roll her in her carriage to the local deli. After I lifted her out and set her in a baby seat, the waitress would tie a bagel around her neck.

Hilary and I walked out to Main Street, then turned into the ice cream shop. We sat down with our cones, and she asked, "Are you coming back on Sunday, like always?"

"Yes, for sure," I said.

A few quick turns and I reached 4th Street to pick up the 10 for the drive to the desert. Once I passed Downtown, it would be a straight shot. With my bag of goodies beside me on the passenger seat, I felt lucky. I had closed a deal on the Landmark Eastern Columbia at the same time as Clifton's. Two deals in the heart of the financial crisis, right before totally running out of money. I was elated. My career and family life were steady, and I was free to detach myself from everything.

I had come to Los Angeles in 1976, shortly after giving up on a college teaching career in New Hampshire because the technical economics required to complete a PhD put me to sleep. I wanted a more romantic, manly career, and spent six years drifting through furniture finishing, cabinet making, and carpentry. But I finally accepted the advice of a carpenter, Loren Evans, who told me as he handed me my last check, "You ain't no carpenter, a cabinet maker maybe, but I doubt it, you better ride that horse in the direction it's going."

I loved Loren Evans and considered him a real man — he ran an all-male construction crew and was assertive, proud, and physically capable — so I took his advice as gospel. I've always been sort of like an empty beach onto which active males would swim up and land. I was always interested in men, not as sexual partners, but as an admirer of their active stances and their proclivities. I wanted to be one. I wanted to know what made them the way they were. And as an empty beach, there were always men landing.

The first whom I loved was Douglas Moore, one of the black kids I met when we moved from the Lower East Side to Rockaway Beach. I had just run a school-yard race and had lost to Eliot Blum, a frail boy in my fourth grade class. After the race, I stood by Eliot and was grimacing at him when Douglas appeared from nowhere and told me in a casual and friendly tone, "If you want to fight him, you have to fight me."

In no time, I decided to skip the battle and befriend the aggressive black stranger. I admired his forward-ness and friendly manner, so when a few months later, he and his brother Terrell trapped me on the street with my shopping cart full of my mother's groceries and pretended to steal them, I knew it was a hoax.

Terrell had rolled the cart away and yelled, "We got your food." But I could tell that confident Douglas was sharing a game with his younger brother. Terrell brought the cart back, and Douglas said, "We were just kidding."

In my teen years, the projects filled up with a pack of new males. Larry Schnitzer stood out. He had come from a tough area of Brooklyn. I met him outside the fence of our junior high school as I was doing my paper route. He stood on the sidewalk in front of me, opened his hands, and motioned in all directions. He regaled me with stories of his fantastic victories against all odds. Dancing in his shiny loafers and carefully pressed slacks, he mimicked a gangster shooting a machine gun. "Crazy Schnitzer" became one of my best friends.

Even though I took the words of the charismatic master carpenter Loren Evans to heart, I had no idea what direction to go. After a few years and a series of dead-end white-collar jobs, I drifted into commercial real estate and got traction in a niche market. Drawn in by the beauty of the abandoned financial district in Downtown Los Angeles, I managed to coexist with a garrulous bunch of ethnic landlords inhabiting the area. At first it was weirder than weird for a former instructor and PhD candidate of a liberal bent to work side-by-side with an avaricious tribe of landlords, but

they trusted me and totally distrusted each other —
and with difficulty, I made deals with them.

Now, I drove by in a string of cars winding along the
rim of the downtown center with the glass-skinned
towers of the financial district off to my left. I told
myself I'd sell one of those sixty-story buildings one
day. The San Gabriel Mountains beyond them hugged
the horizon, and the high-rises looked like children's
toys watched over by a graying grandmother. The
mountains are the ancestors of the basin.

If mother earth were a broker, she might say, "I opened
escrow on the deal twenty-eight million years ago,
when I locked the Pacific Oceanic and North Atlantic
Plates in a grind against each other." When the two
plates locked, friction between them built up until
the earth's crust broke, creating a visible fault and
pushing up mountains. First, the earth's crust has to
move. The heated mantle is thrust upward, building
mountains as the molten rock is released. It took the
San Andreas Fault the twenty-eight million years
to build the rim of ranges in the background of my
two-hour voyage across the basin. The Santa Monica,
San Gabriel, and San Bernardino Mountains. The San
Andreas Fault is still active and heads east, like me,
cracking the earth along its way.

My first date with Nicole, I took her to a Bukowski

play on Traction Avenue where artists were first reclaiming the old lofts. I then dreamt about a woman in a gold lamé blouse and took it as a sign when Nicole wore a gold lamé blouse on our second date. Things moved quickly. Nicole came from a comfortable, down-to-earth family in Beverly Hills. Her mom and dad greeted me warmly.

I was selling a building for a nattily dressed landlord who took me to lunch one day. I told him of my upcoming marriage. "You're getting engaged?" he asked, wiping his mouth. His sapphire cuff links shone in the dim basement. "Ed, get your wife used to the fact that you go away and she doesn't know where you are."

"Okay sure, Frank." I nodded my head.

He walked me up Olive Street and opened the trunk of his Mercedes where he stored a beautifully pressed outfit and full leather set of men's toiletries, always at the ready for his getaways. He winked, "Even if I just want to get hot dogs in Brooklyn."

His advice was valuable to me. He was another real man who had landed on my empty beach. I respected Frank. He was an upscale version of my tough Italian friends in the projects. Once, he locked an entire family of jewelers in his building all night because they wouldn't follow building hours. His words left a mark because I wanted to be like him, but I lost contact with Frank after the deal closed. That happens with a lot of clients. Being discarded like a used condom after a transaction was one of the things that was hard for me, but that wasn't what happened with Frank. He had a heart attack a few months after the deal was done. He was hit hard and wanted me to remember him the way he'd been.

A few years later, Nicole and I were in Palm Springs. We were with another couple, and the husband brought up this great hike he had discovered in his *LA Times*. He suggested we should try it. I loved hiking and agreed right away. I'd been a regular in the Santa Monica Mountains, so I was game for a hike in the desert. When I got into his van, the guy seemed a little full of himself, but I'd been around plenty of guys like that. He explained how there were a few routes we could take. He mentioned how we could pick up Indian Canyon from close to where we were and go through Desert Hot Springs but that it would be better to drive Highway 111 to the freeway. I didn't really care how he went. I was used to men like him making decisions, especially when you're in their van on a trip they suggested, so when he told me we would take the interstate through the San Gorgonio Pass, it sounded fine.

It's a lot easier to take a panoramic view of things when somebody else is in control, and I was enchanted by the startling pieces of desert landscape along the way, starting with the giant San Jacinto and San Gorgonio Mountains we saw on our way to the 10. Route 62 rode a steep incline through hills of green grey shale, the small flat pieces resembled backgammon tiles ready to flip and roll downhill. The road quickly bent east, and in another ten miles we turned off at Joshua Lane and drove into Black Rock Canyon Campground.

Jerry held the map out in front of him as he led us from his van through the continuing display of desert landscapes: a meandering grey wash, then a series of undulating yellow canyons, then a green woods with large fern trees and huge boulders on an angular hillside. The strenuous uphill climb ended when we poked our heads into the air at the top, pulling ourselves onto a large dirt plateau, and saw the gorgeous vista to our south, a wide cobalt sky, the tan sands of Palm Desert, the jade green Coachella Valley, and snow-capped San Jacinto Mountain. I was soul-struck and hardly heard him say, "I'm going to walk ahead to find the other view," as he left my peripheral vision.

For the entire walk down Warren Vista Trail and Black Canyon Wash back to the car, I was silent except for repeated exclamations of, "Wow, that was amazing." Once inside his van for the ride down Route 62, I must have repeated "what a gorgeous view" often enough to make an impression, because when we got back to our wives and stepped from his van, he handed me the article. "I'll probably not go back there," he said, "but you seemed to really like the view, why don't you take this."

"Thanks, Jerry."

Before we rejoined our families, I put it in the trunk of my car. I had fallen in love. I had found my mistress.

For the next eighteen years, when I finished a big deal and needed to get out of Dodge, I hiked to Warren View and recovered that exhilarated state of mind. As Frank had instructed me, I got my wife used to the fact that I went away now and then — without leaving a name, phone number, or address of the place I was going. Every rendezvous, I took off from the Swiss Health Resort in Desert Hot Springs, headed for the Black Rock hike, and spent an afternoon of bliss on the plateau lying in a comfortable perch above the trail and gazing across the Palm Desert at magic San Jacinto.

The *LA Times* article, with its map of the hike, moved with me from my black Saab to a green Jeep Cherokee, then to a black Highlander. On the early encounters, I took the map from the trunk and carried it along, also checking my directions with a compass. But after I learned the route by heart, I stopped using either and left the map behind.

I don't remember seeing it when I organized my things in the rattan baskets.

I passed through undulating Moreno Valley's cobbled hills of sand and grey until I reached the foot of the San Bernardino Mountains — the gorgeous sisters of the San Gabriel range. Lines of patient cars crawled up towards Big Bear and Arrowhead resorts. I continued east towards the haunting wasteland that's been a beacon for dreamers and outcasts for centuries.

In the shadow of monster trucks, my Passat reached the San Gorgonio Pass, the only passageway to and from the high desert in the 1850s for resourceful rustlers who fattened stolen cattle in the high hills of Joshua Tree, then drove them through the pass to markets on the coast. I passed the off-ramp to Palm Springs, where the pass opens to a mile-wide expanse of wavy grasses, rimmed by the brown foothills of the mountains, and dotted by giant wind turbines.

I turned right off the interstate and picked up Route 62 for the short stretch to Desert Hot Springs, pulling off at Indian Canyon to arrive at Swiss Health Resort, the same restful place I always stayed. The lot in the rear was uncrowded on the hot afternoon, and after a few rings on the buzzer, still nobody came to open the motel registration room. Then finally, ruddy-looking Ursula, the proprietor, came up the steps from her private rooms to greet me.

"Hello, Ed. So nice to see you."

"Same here." I sat on a couch as she went behind the counter to get my paperwork. She was writing up my bill. "So, when is breakfast?" I asked.

"So sorry, Ed. We stopped offering breakfast."

"Not enough visitors this weekend?'

"We're not set up for it anymore, with the financial crisis, and some of the regulars stopped. But I just baked some multigrain bread; if you like, I can get a loaf."

"Sure." I nodded.

She went back to her place, and I recalled Ursula's busy breakfasts in past decades — I saw people waiting to fill up on Swiss Muesli, hard-boiled eggs, fresh vegetables, and colorful jams of berries and prickly pear. As I wondered when exactly was the last time I was there, the smell of her wonderful multigrain bread came in. It distracted me from telling her where I was going the next morning. "Here you are." She handed me the bread and bent her silver head over the paperwork, wrote the $5.00 bread charge to my total, and addressed me from inside her space. "Karl is still doing the water-massage, would you like that?"

"That sounds good." I had never tried his special massage in all the visits to the place. It sounded like a fantastic way to start the weekend and might actually wash the last buyers off my skin.

"He has a 7 p.m. opening. Is that good?"

I floated face up in the indoor pool on that Thursday night buoyed by multicolor noodles. Karl stepped into the water and greeted me politely, but without any warmth, in his Swiss accent: "You're here for a one-hour water massage?"

"Yes, I am," I answered, knowing how relaxing it would be. The tall, muscular man walked behind me to cradle me in his arms and began to massage my back. He carried me to the center of the warm pool.

"Do you like firm massage?"

"Yes." His stiffness impressed me. It's not like he hadn't seen me fifteen times before. Or hadn't talked to me about the special access his property had to the underground hot springs. But I knew I was in for a treat. I thought about the Allstate Insurance ad, "You're in good hands," and I closed my eyes. His finger tips pressed across my waistline from hip to hip, then he massaged my back, moving upward and outward from my spine. I went into a reverie. I imagined myself leaving my room in the morning to take my car up Route 62. I'd reach the campground parking lot, and, dressed in my shorts and short sleeves, would tackle the familiar trail, finding my way from the black-pebbled channel to the yellow grasslands and up to the green forest for the view. I saw myself eating lunch nestled in a crag above the trail, across from San Jacinto and the Coachella Valley. Then, I would drive back, and everything would be like always, a blue-sky feeling on the pool deck of the resort.

Karl and Ursula had invested in new beds and bedding. I pulled back the coral and yellow weaved covers and untucked the lower edge of the fine cotton sheets from beneath the mattress. My travel bag lay unopened on the second bed. I set out my outfit for the hike: my hiking socks, short sleeve white shirt, underwear, and shorts. I cut two thick slices off Ursula's luscious bread and slathered both with crunchy peanut butter, then gingerly placed these together, cut the sandwich in half, and wrapped it in aluminum foil. Ursula had left several delicious tomatoes on the kitchen counter. I took one and put it in the fridge in a plastic bag with the peanut butter sandwich. It was close to 10 p.m. when I filled a glass with some cold goat milk and then finished off half a bag of Sara Lee Bordeaux cookies. When I closed my eyes and pulled just the right layer of sheets and coverlet over me, the last thing I noticed was my box of granola, next to the sink, waiting for morning on the kitchen counter.

For all my anticipation of a wonderful day, I woke on Friday morning very weak in the already warm room. Once my feet reached the floor by the bed, I ran to the bathroom with cramps from diarrhea. At 7 a.m., yellow morning light illuminated the asphalt lot. At its edges, the view of grey desert gravel and scraggly grass was very unmotivating. My mind agreed with my body's weakness, and despite the months of anticipation, I told myself "forget the hike," flipped on the swamp cooler, crept under the covers, and slept.

Two hours later, my cell phone woke me up. It was Britten, a client. We had circled beneath every beaux-arts facade and each goddess and gargoyle of the historic core, as if we were Jason and the Argonauts in search of the Golden Fleece, and we'd still not found him a deal. When he realized he had awakened me, he suggested we talk later. Foggy, I stumbled around the room. It was around 10 a.m., and if I were to take the hike, I was two hours behind schedule, but I decided to go. I threw on my outfit. I left the box of granola untouched, opened the fridge and filled a glass with peach juice from Trader Joe's. The glass slipped from my hand, and I watched shards disperse on the linoleum. I bent to mop up the little glass islands from the peach sea. Standing, I tossed the paper towels in the trash, then grabbed my peanut butter sandwich and tomato and headed to the parking lot, determined to reach the gorgeous vista.

I stopped for coffee. After grabbing a styrofoam cup to fill, I noticed a family in the front window nook at a white formica table. The waitress had just brought some sunny side up eggs on white plates with bacon. She leaned over the bony-armed father to pour his coffee. The t-shirted man smiled at his son, and the buxom wife in a work shirt beamed at the kid. I turned back to the vat and flicked up the dispenser. The waitress behind the restaurant grill window asked me, "Anything else you want?"

"No, but where is the cream?"

"There is some milk over there." She pointed to a jar of powdered milk on a high shelf. I scraped the crust off the powder top, then mixed some in my coffee. My eyes were drawn to the family in the nook near the door. To avoid them seeing me seeing them, I focused my attention on the brass staples circling the backs of the red Naugahyde chairs. They matched the metal-buttoned suspenders on the man's jeans. The waitress in her white apron brought the family English muffins. The man buttered his, and I watched the melting gold fill the crusty crannies before he dipped it in his pooling orange yolk. He savored the egg and smiled to his wife as if he had sold The Bank of America Towers. With my neck craned over, to keep an eye on the family, I waited for the waitress to return from her conversation with the man working the grill in the kitchen, then asked, "How much for the coffee?"

"$1.50."

I carried the foam cup in front of me, down the center of the café, and as I opened the door by their niche, the wife said, "Sure, Honey," to a request from the little boy and leaned forward to stick a bacon strip into his mouth.

I continued up Route 62. After miles of broken windows and shuttered storefronts, I reached Route 248, the west entrance to Joshua Tree National Park and Black Rock Canyon Campground. The access road led to the ranger station, where I usually parked. The wooden building had a sign that read, "Park Closed," but cars had filled the spots.

I drove down to the regular parking lot, which was packed, and after searching for a spot, I saw an old, bearded guy standing by his trailer.

"Hi, I'm on a day hike. Do you know a place I can park?"

"Right there is okay. I've seen hikers leave their car in that place."

"Thanks, that's great."

I pulled my Passat into the dirt across from his red trailer. The kind of space you would not know is there until you make it. Heat hung over the lot. Knowing it would be even hotter as the day wore on, I was in a rush to get going. It was hot enough to leave my jacket in the trunk. I glanced at the red and blue water jugs in my new wicker containers, but I was in a hurry and figured that I had enough in the camelback for the usual three-hour hike.

I stepped away from the silver trunk onto the sand and strapped on my pack. Still a little sleepy, even after the coffee, I asked a last question of the white-beard, "Hey, can you remind me where the access trail is to Warren View?"

"Sure." The helpful man pointed thirty yards away.

It was close to 1 p.m. I strolled up an incline from the campground to the road, and the familiar white water tower appeared behind the trail. West on the dirt road to the trailhead, I kept a steady pace until a brown and tan coyote stepped out of the scrub and met me. Instead of circling to avoid contact, it planted its paws in my path. The trailhead sign was visible between his ears, almost as if he were park property.

For the first time in two decades, a coyote was blocking my way to Warren View. Its black snout ten feet away. The brown-tinged auburn fur against the brown twigs of the desert. The narrow eyes above the white chin. We stood in the heat above the beige and green tents in the campground. He seemed to address me. Me, in my white short-sleeve shirt and beige shorts, the coyote in its beige fur, tinged with white.

It was late midday toward the end of September; any hikers would already be well into their hikes. We stood and waited. The auburn fur on his hump rumpled in a warm breeze. I leaned on my hiking stick, watched until the creature turned and crossed the high weeds behind it. Its bushy tail left the road and blended with the white buds of dried borage and disappeared. I headed to the trailhead.

The trailhead sign came up in fifty yards on the left side of the access road, and I crossed over to take it at about 1:15 p.m. I planned to be back at my car by 4:30 p.m. The familiar sandy trail was lined with dried shrubs and succulents, and after about a quarter mile it reached Black Rock Canyon Wash, where the trail started in earnest. I stepped down into the forty-yard-wide, pebbled channel and, out of habit, turned right. I didn't need to reconnoiter or correlate my direction to any compass point. The wash didn't have a drop of water in it. Lined by a landscape of short grasses and rocks, shriveled purple prickly pear blossoms, and dried yucca wands that had sprouted in spring, the wash broadened and shrunk as it rose on a gradual incline for about a mile.

After a mile, the wash passed a set of ramshackle water tanks made of large rocks which settlers used to collect water and feed cattle, and where I had a memory of my daughter calling me five years earlier and proudly announcing, "Dad, I passed my driver's test finally," as I dreaded the day she would actually be on the road. At the same place where the tanks sit, the wash turned steep and dragged on my ankles as it narrowed to about thirty yards across.

I stepped along on the steeper gradient still inside the wash, the only change being that I was conscious of the drag on my boots and pebbles falling off each time I lifted my foot, leaving deeper footprints in the sand. A half-mile past the rock tanks, I reached a familiar change in the landscape, yellow grass hills no more than fifty feet tall. The trail continued uphill on a looping dirt track weaving through a series of narrow canyons all inhabited by brittle scraggly weeds. Occasional Joshua trees lined the dunes. The hot sun hung in front of me but disappeared inside the relief of each canyon. The rock trail disappeared at times, when my footsteps led directly into one of the grassy hills, but I knew from past trips to continue circling through the maze in the general direction of the sun. After a half mile of circling through the maze, I reached a fork in the road with signs to Warren Vista and Warren View.

The air was stale and hot with a small breeze. The heat was excessive, though the lid on my hat kept the glare from my face. As always, I chose the sign to the right towards Warren View. The trail steepened a bit and continued up for a hundred yards then ramped up a green hillside, where the grass hunched close to the ground, woven into sparse patches alongside large white boulders, fir trees, and junipers. The trip up the steep, wooded hill took twenty minutes. At the top, I arrived at a plateau under a large sky with a row of trees at its extreme edge. My heart raced. It felt so good to be closing in on my cherished view of San Jacinto. But I also felt some time pressure. I rushed along what was left of the trail, an indistinct footpath twirling through the foot-high, windblown grasses of the plateau.

A gray cone of stones and dirt appeared. At about one-hundred-feet tall, it was the dominant feature of the landscape before me, and it would make the perfect point from which to view San Jacinto. I stepped through the indistinct grass path without paying much attention until I saw a sign I'd never seen before. A hundred yards beyond the cone, in that row of trees at the far edge of the plateau, the sign read "West Trail." I walked ahead to the high, conical pile, but when I got there, I was still confused by the sign. I walked past the cone and craned my neck left to search for the West Trail sign on the line of trees but saw nothing. I gave up the search for the black and white letters, walked back to the cone-shaped pile, and took my first steps up.

I had never mounted this cone to see Warren View, and having never seen this formation before, the steep angle of incline surprised me. Loose stones and dirt rolled out from under the pressure of my boots. Then my cell phone rang. A co-worker. I watched my step and let the call go to voicemail. Treading with care on the unstable ground, I reached a spot where two grey rocks stuck from the hillside, making a chair. The last few steps made me feel the mid-day heat more than the previous two miles. I took the pack from my back and squeezed my hips into the one-foot-wide "chair," caught my breath, and sat to admire the Palm Desert expanse, snow-capped San Jacinto Peak, and the jade-green Coachella Valley.

I pulled my lunch out from the outer pocket of my pack. I sat down in the crevice with relief. I sprinkled salt on the fresh red and yellow tomato and sunk my jaws in. The peanut butter on fresh baked bread was next. I licked the excess off the crusts and savored each bite of the sandwich. I took a long sip, nearly emptying the camelback.

A rock tumbled down the cone. My seat was precariously high on a peak under the cerulean sky, across from the white crown of San Jacinto. Ending my reverie, awake to the heat, I stood up and shuffled around, settling the orange pack on my back as pebbles slipped from under my feet. After establishing my balance, I placed each step carefully, feeling for loose rocks under my boots, and threaded my way down the cone to the level plane of short grasses.

Safely off the rocky cone, I walked to the sandy hint of trail that I had taken across the plateau. I followed it through yellowed clumps of grass on a gradual down-hill curve, expecting to reach the forest of pines and large boulders below. But after a hundred yards or so, I found myself amidst multiple short paths circling the grass, but I couldn't see a clear trail weaving through. I scanned the ground for a trail, but found nothing. I needed a marker in the landscape. My throat was itchy; the air had heated up. The sweatband on my hat was damp and dripped on my forehead. I needed to find the shade of the woods and then down and out of Black Rock Canyon, but there were no footprints of any kind, not even my own.

As I searched for prints, I remembered the last circuit I had made to Warren View. My anxiety level increased as I recalled I had followed a bunch of locals all the way, after one had stuck his head out from the water tanks at the beginning of the hike and offered to take me on a route to the local view of Warren Peak. I remembered that hike with the mismatched group of eight, some in shorts and sneakers, others in hiking gear. The recollection brought my eyes to the boulders rising from the yellow grass a few hundred yards away, where they had led me. I hoped to find footprints at their outlook. I crossed the plateau to the circle of rocks where I had sat with that raucous bunch.

Searching the sands in front of the boulders for footprints, I recalled the young military vet in a camouflage jacket yelling, "Hey, you faggots, can't you find the trail? You guys are locals, right?" I remembered us on vague grass paths, him calling out repeatedly, "No, not over there, that goes nowhere." Or, "Come on, I don't want to tell your mamma I left you at Warren View." With his words echoing in my mind, I searched the rock circle for prints, hoping some locals like those guys had just been there. I would then follow the tracks through the woods to the yellow hills, the dried riverbed, and my car.

There was not a single mark on the dry ground. It was hotter than it had been when I started at noon. I had no more water. I paced back and forth, searching the ground for footprints in a fifty-yard arc between the spot where I lost the trail and the rock circle of the locals. Nothing!

I thought that if I found the "West Trail" sign, it might be a reckoning point. From there, I would retrace my steps to the water bottles in my trunk, and head to the motel, but between the rocky conical hill and inside the row of green firs that lined the edge of the plateau, there was no sign. The sun continued to burn. Grasses, prickly pear cactus, and creosote bushes, nothing else. My mouth itched, and I was now desperate to find my way back.

Through an opening in the dense underbrush, a channel a foot high and a few feet wide cut the edge of the plateau in one spot. I stepped cautiously into the sloped cutout. It was difficult to make out the ground below through tubular weeds and cactus, but I craned my neck for a view and saw a pebbled trail on a landing ten feet down. I disentangled myself from the spines of a prickly pear cactus, which had attached itself to my backpack, its purple fruit swung back into place, and I stepped out to the ledge of the ditch to peer at the trail below. A turkey buzzard chanced an air current into the distant desert, and I stopped squirming inside the ditch. I found my resolve and took off my pack, then threw it over the edge onto the dirt, sent my hiking stick out ahead of it, and jumped.

II.

THE ORANGE PACK cushioned my landing. The height of vertical rock and dirt between the plateau and ground showed how far I had let myself fall. The knee-high grey stones, lime green shrubs, and the tiny hedge-hog cacti were familiar. I was inside the landscape I'd viewed from above. Rolling tan hills sloping down to the basin; I had no choice but to follow the path downhill. I imagined guys I knew from my old company walking beside me — Phil Sample had a shoulder pack filled with guns and knives; Larry Wass carried survivalist gear from his four-wheeler. We circled down the first bend, leaving the woods for the drier grass canyons.

The nearby brown hills opened and closed until the path reached an incline lined with red barrel cactus and a series of globular boulders. I walked one hundred feet up the lopsided path, and stood alongside these giant rocks. The rim of my hat was barely level with their midpoints. With three multi-colored boulders clustered around, it looked like God the pinball wizard had stopped in the middle of the match. It was an enchanting sight, and the fantasy of my muscular companions evaporated.

I stepped past the boulders, lit copper by the hot sun, and was on the ledge of a sandy plateau. My throat itched. I scratched my tongue to peel off gunky residue. After a hundred yards through short grass and creosote, the plateau ended abruptly with a deep fifteen-foot drop-off. I'd almost been mid-air. I noticed to my right someone had built a tapered pile of stones. This was encouraging — this cracked landscape was still a hiking trail. Hell-bent to get to the parking lot, I decided to tie my emergency rope to the marker and use it as an anchor to lower myself down. It took a few minutes to unpack the fresh yellow nylon from its cellophane wrappings because I had never used it before.

I sat in my yellow tie and itchy Cub Scout uniform at a quarter after five.

"I hear your Dad coming off the elevator, and your meeting already started," Mom warned.

"I hate the Cub Scouts," I whined. "I can't stand all those stupid knots and this uniform."

My father came in and slapped my face.

"Why didn't you go to the Cub Scouts?"

"I hate them!" I cried into my itchy blue shirt.

Pondering the puzzle of which slap dash knot to use to fasten my rope to the marker in order to hold my weight as I lowered myself down, I could see myself falling backwards fifteen feet and bashing my skull as the rope tore loose. With that vision in mind, I was desperate for an alternative. To my left there was a jagged bunch of black, glassy rocks that extended into the airspace over the drop. There was a convex saddle in the middle. Overall it looked to be a safer launch from there than lowering myself down backwards on an uncertain knot. I left the yellow cord dangling, telling myself, "In case I am lost, my rope will be a good signal to rescuers."

I climbed up the black rocks to sit in the saddle, then hovered over the dirt twenty feet below. With a smooth stone in my mouth, I sucked to relieve my throat. No saliva. After looking back and forth, back and forth from the dangling yellow rope to where I sat on the shiny launching platform, I threw my pack out into the dirt, followed again by my stick and myself. This landing was more forceful than my initial jump from the ridge of trees, and I slid forward a few feet as the sand absorbed the impact. I seemed to be on a lateral surface, but suddenly it all changed to a forty-five-degree slope of dried yuccas and firs. The sun was tilted to the hillside, the hillside was askew to the sky. I looked back and could not see the marker with my rope or the craggy black saddle. "You don't belong here," I thought. Unable to walk upright, I sat down and slid, zigzagging down the dirt slope using plants and my stick as brakes. Each time I got close to a plant, I dug the stick into the dirt to protect myself from impact. Then I let myself slide to the next plant and then the next, until I came to a stop at a white boulder, my legs and back scratched from unplanned encounters with hidden thorns. I stretched myself flat across the boulder for a view.

More dirt and rocks below, hemmed by sand. Joshua trees poked out at weird angles. I saw a draw where men on horseback would assist me. Cowboys would pull me up on a saddle and ride me home. I only had to get there. I looked for a way, but there was no way down, short of jumping off.

I got into the dirt, in front of the boulder, leaned over the plateau and flung my pack and stick onto the sand below. I would have to throw myself a few feet out in a Hail Mary pass to clear the protruding rocks and shrubs of the lumpy hillside. I outstretched my hands while leaping toward the bright orange mark and closed my eyes. I landed, held onto the pack to keep from rolling over, and stood on the narrow strip. We had left a six-foot-wide impression in the sand.

There was only to continue, so I walked left on the narrow strip of sand and checked the area where I had imagined a trail and cowboys who might emerge to save me, but there was only a crowded thicket of blackened shrubs. Only miniature cowboys on horseback would fit through. To my right, the sand strip continued at a steep angle downward. I crept on all fours along the scary down slope of the rim of sand until it reached a two-hundred-foot-high mound of loose dirt and scraggly plants, then turned even more sharply downward to its left. I poked my head in the shrubs to see further below and felt like a shrunken trapped Alice. Shards of white rock and wood debris repeated themselves as they descended a long brown and green precipice punctuated by a series of sand landings.

Whatever this was, it was not a hiking trail. Whatever had happened to me had happened so quickly and irreversibly. I needed a way off the vortex of falling earth, rock, and twisted vegetation. My only way forward was the unstable mound of debris to my right. Above its crown, a little trail seemed to snake down the hills beyond. Putting my pack back on, I took my first steps up the dirt hill, which was speckled with hedge hogs and dried brown ocotillo, their shrunken black buds on split stems ready to flop on the unsettled soil. But stand they did, and the more I lost my footing and fell on the upward climb, the more my admiration for them grew. To keep from falling, I took rigid, calculated steps and crisscrossed the mound in martial arts triangles of stick and two legs. I littered the basin with screams of "Fuck you, Chuck," my former corporate boss, and like an Energizer

Bunny of hate, reached the top.

My hunch was right! From the top, I saw that the pebbled trail reached the bottom of my mound of debris and continued downhill. I had a moment of gratitude. I only had to get to the trail, but the down slope of the pile of scraggly thorns, pebbles, and dirt was long and steep.

It wasn't my plan, but as it happened, I went down like a piece of detritus, like rock and dirt that blows, drains, and falls to its resting place, Wallace Stegner's "angle of repose" in the Western landscape. I was a limp rag doll collapsing into the hill at the beginning of each new effort. My pack shielded my back, but cacti scratched my arms and legs with each flip of my torso. Finally, nature put some skin in the game and offered a sandstone bend at the bottom of the hill. I slid comfortably over its edge and plopped down onto the pebbled road, sighing "Thank God," and feeling absolutely positive that I was bound for the parking lot.

Now it was over, I was sure. I stood up, then walked along the stable four-foot-wide road of gravel and sand that looked like a new interstate highway compared to the "trail" I had escaped. The orange pack ruffled across my back in unison with my steps as the uniform grey road broadened and stayed level. Passing a pastoral-looking patch of green grasses, where a flock of desert pheasant whooshed off hurriedly, I imagined

I'd soon reach the trunk of my car and lift the red water bottle to my lips. But the path reached a fork. The left side went ten feet and ended in a set of deep tire grooves, as if a truck had stopped there dead in its tracks. The tire tracks were encrusted with pebbles that looked like they had been stuck there for months, indicating it was no busy highway, but since I was searching for a path out of my predicament, and could not afford to overlook any alternative, I went ahead to check past the deep imprints. Seeing the path dead-end in a line of shrubs fifty feet away, I returned to the fork and followed the right side. My mind forced me to turn repeatedly back toward the fork, and each time I did so, felt sharp chest pains. When the tracks disappeared from view, I stopped asking myself if I had made the wrong choice. The trail rolled along as it stabilized to become a ten-foot-wide arroyo or dried creek. I stepped on the black and gray pebbles inside the ditch, eye-level with the scraggly weeds lining its sides, and descended a gradual grade for maybe ten minutes.

I found myself in a broad, exposed maze of shallow flood channels alongside a stretch of limestone cliffs. Everything was white in the late afternoon. The dusty road was powdery. The sun flashed in my face when I tried to look at the distant hills. My mouth was dry, and I sucked with all my might on the camelback tube.

I pressed 911 on my cell phone. Never an answer.

My wife's voice and my rejoinders repeated like bird songs; "Why don't you just stay in the pools? They say a heat wave is hitting the Mojave this weekend, you sure it's a good time for the desert?"

"Yes, Honey, you know I've been doing this forever.... Honey, don't worry it's the same hike I always take."

"Maybe you should just stay in the pools and relax." At the foot of the stairs my wife's voice trailed off in the kitchen.

I was without water. There was a flash of color in a limestone crevice ahead, and I imagined a hiker in a flannel shirt of violet and red, but when I reached the spot, only a dried prickly pear, a creased blossom, a shrunken survivor of the hundred-degree heat greeted me. Turning from the blackened blossom, I thought back to the coyote and wished he had kept his black snout in my face all day so I wouldn't be out in this eerie space of white road, sky, and endless hills.

When the trail left the white cliffs for a natural arena of black boulders, I collapsed in gratitude. Sitting in their shadows, I noticed a set of bicycle grooves in a darker, once moist patch of sand fronting the rocks, and realized that neighborhood kids played there. I remembered the nook of the bacon-chomping boy and his family at the diner, so I waited for him and his dad to drive down from the hills in an older, well-used, black pick-up. I could see the dad's slim, muscular arms extended in front of him, comfortable on the steering wheel, the boy smiling, his bike behind them in the open cab, next to his dad's metal toolbox.

A light shone off the chrome bumper in my vision of the man's truck. I moved my hand to cover my eyes and woke in the truck-less rock warren. My pack, lying between my boots on the sand, felt very heavy when I threw it on my back and stepped out of the shadows, onto the dusty path. I walked towards the sun, which threw a shade off the rim of my hat down to my lips. Each time I lifted my head to check it, the white torch seemed suspended off a further ridge of the distant ranges visible from the ridge of trees. As my path crossed other arroyos intermittently, I stepped along, occasionally dislodging a gray, black, or red pebble with my boots.

My solar orientation was secure, but my visibility was blocked by cholla cacti and shrubs taller than me, even the occasional bristles of Joshua trees, and by hills lining the sides of the long plain. Every half mile or so, in the cracked ground of arroyo intersections, loopy limbed cholla stood in rock piles with red barrel cacti. The plants glowed with gorgeous orange light gathered in their spines. They were as tall as cowboys, and their supple limbs took on assorted shapes. Long, curved limbs were cowboys twirling ropes. Smaller loops were their smiling faces watching a lost hiker going by. One sat in a large split rock and played cards on the red barrel tables.

Each time I reached one of the cholla hangouts, it felt good to see them, as if they were kids on my tag team in the projects, as if the long stretches of desert sand were the paved walkways and the cholla hangout was the safe tree by the kids' park. They were my friends as I rushed downhill through two miles worth of arroyos in a half hour, almost as fast as the flash floods that made them, those swarms of mud and rock that never found an exit from the basin, and neither would I.

After endless looping, the mazes converged in a flat, broad road. The sandy cliffs stood back from the clear highway, which was obviously built for heavy use, and I was encouraged that I'd see a person or vehicle. For a moment, the sagebrush scent and the open sky felt good. A hundred yards on, a few huge pieces had broken from the hillsides. The sight of the fallen giants briefly distracted me from my plight as I thought of bankrupt developers jumping off buildings downtown, but after several miles of my solitary footprints on the dusty barren road with its white heat reflecting on my face, I was desperate for an exit.

Then a large hill appeared a mile ahead; it looked

like a turn off. "It must go to the local neighborhood," I surmised. Looking up at a friendly guy on his horse, I'd ask, "Where is the intersection with the road to the parking lot?" I hurried over. Closing in on what from a distance looked like a hundred-foot-high, gumdrop shaped bump, I saw it was a large dirt and rock hill, hundreds of feet high, which the pebbled road then straddled.

There was no exit sign. Instead, my eyes were led upward as the road climbed a steep grade that wound along the hill's contours. After a few circumnavigations, I looked back and saw my long afternoon path was a thin brown line on the desert floor. My fears returned. A rock terrace at the apex of the road presented an endless view of dimpled desert and distant ranges, as if it were built as an attraction for lost tourists.

I continued on the path beyond the terrace, continued my search for an escape from the grueling heat, but within ten yards, the road abruptly cut through a ledge of purple granite shards, cutting through my own being as well, as I entered a precious way station and the feeling of search turned to one of arrival. I stopped moving. The sound of the hot breeze off the basin disappeared. I was on a fine sand floor enclosed within three cliffs studded with striated slabs in every shade of rose. The arid air soothed my spirits. The harsh cliff faces softened my being. My mind shut down. Like a child at a beach, I bent to feel the talcum sands in my fingers.

Alongside the lavender slabs above me, pistachio agave blades grew from the walls like cathedral florets. Curls of green grass filled the dry water cracks like wallpaper. My body turned from the weary bones of a hiker to an extension of the sand, granite, and sky. The puzzle of the lopsided landscape, the hill of thorns, and the wandering trails had no answer. I had arrived at my sanctuary. I named it "Purple Canyon." I stood there, a child looking up at its teacher.

The craggy faced Elizabeth B. Moon found me scribbling at my desk. "I see you like poetry, Edward." The edges of her puritanical face softened in the sunlight of the sixth-grade classroom windows. She towered over me in her black dress. "Here is a book I think you will like." She handed me a black book; on its cover, gold embossed letters said "Bullfinch's Mythology."

"Edward, would you like to run the science table?"

"Yes, Mrs. Moon."

I sat at my little metal-legged desk and considered how to fill the doubled-sized science table. I went to the library and brought back colored science and exploration books.

"That looks good, Edward. I think the other

students will like your table."

"Really, Mrs. Moon?"

"Yes, of course."

My throat itched. I was out of water, and my cell battery was dead. The sun threatened the sky. A full daytime moon hung on the lip of the canyon. I turned from it to continue over a slight rise and downhill toward the old man's spot with my Passat. I needed the red and blue water bottles in the trunk. I felt for my car key and left the enchanted place, the talcum path descended, and the ground coarsened with a mix of pebbles and broken rock. The place I had named "Purple Canyon" was almost out of view. I passed a stretch of large, grey, rounded boulders and wondered if these isolated giants guarded that magic place. The trail wound down to a landscape of sand mounds and small plateaus. In a flat area, the bleached carcass of a big horn sheep appeared. The horns hovered half a foot above the jaw bone. The outline of the face was clear. The spine curved from the jaw to the tail bone. Two legs were missing. Two were askew, as if it was just knocked over and its flesh evaporated.

Nicole and I, on a hike in Anza Borrego, had followed the sound of water to the oasis and sat in the shade, listening to the barking of frogs. Palm fronds waved above the small pond. Tiny gold-colored desert fish were visible in the water. We watched a butterfly land on a pistachio-green weed. I was proud of her. She didn't take desert hikes with me. It hadn't been easy for her to climb over the large tan boulders, or to follow the winding path that entered the darkened alcove. I pulled our lunches out of my pack, and we chomped down on sandwiches beneath the palm fronds and drank water with abandon.

We sighted two big horn sheep, rock steady on a steep angle of a rock terrace. I said, "That's fantastic — see, I told you we would get lucky."

"They're so beautiful, wow. That lady we met said she had been here ten times and never saw one."

When we finished lunch, I reminded her, "We have to go down the way we came up, first threading the curves and then over the boulders." We stepped carefully off the muddy platform of the green oasis into the sun and held hands down the steep curves to the lower trail. As we walked out on a smooth rock ledge, we came upon an entire family of big horn sheep.

The healthy, plump, wool-covered sheep did not leave the ledge. No other hikers were near. The black noses in the white muzzles didn't twitch. The narrow eyes didn't open wide. The huge segmented horns of the two males bowed gently as they nibbled the grass on the rim of the ledge. We stood there silent, until the group turned their backsides to us and nimbly ascended the cliffs.

I moved on with my head swiveling back every few yards to check the skeleton. The bones looked like a chalk-on-sand stick figure drawn as a warning to lost hikers. The once living sheep disappeared as the trail descended to a lopsided landscape of dunes, well-formed piles of sand dropped by Mother Nature as she drained detritus off the little San Bernardino Mountains.

It looked so much like a beach, it made me smile at the memory of my mom and our summers in Rockaway Beach, and I could almost see her limping across these dunes with her polio-weakened leg as she did there, and then discarding her brace at the mythical ocean and jumping in.

But I was not in Rockaway, and these dunes were detritus descending. I had become the lost hiker, who four hours earlier didn't fill his camelback from the red and blue water bottles in the new rattan containers he had bought the day before at Bed Bath & Beyond, where he reorganized the trunk of his silver car in the parking lot. A hiker who ignored a warning from a coyote and didn't use the red and white compass in his pocket when he jumped down off the plateau in a gamble to return to a different parking lot.

That path had led him to jump off a perch of glassy black rocks, hurl himself onto a narrow cliff face, and tumble through a hill of thorns. As he descended the dunes, the path was a mystery. The full moon hung on his shoulder as the sun above the distant mountains slipped in and out of view. After much meandering, the ramshackle piles tightened up on both sides of him and, at twice his height, forced him into a narrow corridor no wider than the fifth floor of Clifton's Cafeteria leading to the bakery. He was led to a smooth rock slide, like a child's water chute, and feeling like the child who made the science table and the boy who saw his cowboy cholla in the arroyos, he slid down. At the bottom, he leaned his face against the cool pink stone. Surprised at how far he had slid, he told himself, "I can never get back up this thing if I have to."

The bajada broadened and undulated downhill. The alluvium was interrupted by a series of ridges as the desert reproduced itself in every direction. On both sides of the trail, brittle bunch grasses lay, dark green rings of creosote leaves huddled against the sun, and on the lost hiker's flanks, bristled Joshua trees protruded at awkward angles from identical sandy cliffs. He felt like a man attached to a mile-square treadmill with a desert painted on it. Each time he walked up and over a ridge, he found himself facing a duplicate.

"Will you tell me about the mountains over there?" The eleven-year-old boy, beside him in the rear seat, asked, "Why are they grey?"

"What?"

"Why do they look grey, but when we get close, they have colors."

"Everything is like that. From far away they seem plain and simple, but up close, you see how complicated it is," he answered. Satisfied, the boy turned back to the grey blue hills in the distance. The boy's mother, who had picked up the hitchhiker on the road back from Istanbul said, "We are stopping in a few places before Athens. Would you like to join us?"

"That would be great!"

After two days of lamb and salad meals and restful sleep in clean motels — "Stay in touch," said the husband. He handed the hitchhiker their Brazilian address.

The lost hiker remembered the boy's sad goodbye. And he remembered his own words, "... up close you see how complicated it is."

He faced the same ridges he'd first seen from the plateau, all the way from the weird kaleidoscope of deadly jumps and his escape via the hill of debris. And the long hours he used to cross the intersecting arroyos, which led him to the purple canyon. He had been chasing the sun over those ridges since 2 p.m. and hadn't gotten any closer to an exit in four hours. And, a mile or so into the reproducing desert he now noticed that the plants alongside him were blacker, and the creosote was sharing the ground with a thick brush he hadn't seen before. The basin he was descending took on a bleached look and broadened on both sides. "Oh my God," he said to himself, "This is some fucking hike, I'm headed into the Sonoran Desert." I lay down in the shadow of a friendly boulder.

It was the summer before my first year in high school. A new housing project had been built across Beach Channel Drive and co-ops had been put up on 56th Street, alongside the playground. We were just getting to know all the new kids who had moved to Rockaway. I was already friends with two of them, Gary and Gordon, and we were playing three-man knock-around softball when I first saw her.

I went to catch up with a long drive Gordon had hit when I saw the girl on the playground bench. She was there alone, just sitting in a short skirt. She was different from the girls in the projects. None of them would sit around alone like that. She wasn't well taken care of. I could tell right away the girl wasn't one of the new girls in Rockaway. The new girls in the co-op had money and dressed nice. And the new project girls were mostly black and from the south. None of those girls came over alone, and they were church-type nice girls. I had a paper route in the new projects, and I had never run across this white girl there. She was probably from the shanties on the bay side of the peninsula.

There were a lot of leftovers like her, from before the projects went up. Like Barish, who I met when I was shopping for my mom at the food store past the elevated train line. He was white and rough looking like her. He was drunk with a bottle in his hand when he stumbled across my shopping cart. Holding onto the cart he told me, "My Dad got me a hooker when I was old enough to fuck." He then went on to use the n-word. I had pulled the cart back and stared at him in revulsion as he continued, "My Dad got her a six-pack and brought her there." He pointed to the busted-up bungalows on the streets closer to the beach.

I left the knock-around softball game with Gary and Gordon and walked to the bench. I sat down next to her in the shade of the fences and said hello. Her red hair was messy, and the skin on her face was rough, but she was sexy. Her legs were pretty smooth, and she only had one or two bruises on her calf. She had cheap shoes on that hadn't been polished. I wanted to walk her to the streets near the beach and take her into an empty place and make out with her. I looked through the fence and under the trestles, toward the bleached-out bungalows and streets filled with broken bottles. I pointed in the direction of the beach and said, "It's really nice by the ocean." The girl nodded. I noticed how pretty her eyes were. She said, "Yeah."

I should have asked her right then to leave with me, but I wasn't used to asking girls things like that. Behind my back at the opposite fence of the big playground Gary yelled out, "Ed, are you playing?" I waved him off behind me. The girl smiled at me, and I smiled back. I could see to my right that a bunch of other guys I knew were walking over. One of them yelled, "Hey, Eddie, what are you doing?" The others laughed. They came around the bench. A couple of them squeezed into the space behind the bench and held to the wooden slats on both sides of the girl and me.

"What are you doing?' one asked.

I said, "We're going for a walk."

"Oh, can we go too?"

I tried to wave them off. But they were giddy and wouldn't stop making jokes to each other and laughing. I should have gotten up and walked away with the girl, if I knew her better, or if I was more experienced at this type of thing. Instead, the girl got up and walked out of the park. The boys shut up and walked away.

I was furious. I had never been really angry in my life until that day. I went to join up with Gary and Gordon at the opposite fence and started screaming "Fuck you" to both of them before I was even halfway there. Gary looked at me incredulous, and said, "Take shortstop, and Gordon will hit some grounders to you. I'll play first base."

"Fuck you, motherfucker," I yelled.

Gary went over to Gordon, and they huddled. "Were not playing with you," Gordon said. "Go sit down."

I sat, hit the back of my head on the boulder and woke.

The only way I'd see my wife and daughter again was to put everything into reverse. The moon had hung on my shoulder since Purple Canyon, and now I turned to follow her up the long bajada to that magic place, and then I would retrace my way across the arroyos and to the tire track. I told myself that the tire track must lead to a trail that I had missed before and started the voyage up the miles-long plain of sandy ridges as the words of my hiking buddy Barry rang in my ear, "What goes down must come up."

After a mile or so, it must have been 7 p.m. and the full moon, which had been a small oval over Purple Canyon, became a giant searchlight. It hovered on the bajada and led me to a silver landscape of glowing mineral traces. The sky was a violet blanket. I dropped into a little runnel, a perfect place to sleep, about fifty yards wide, sheltered on all sides. The runnel was a flat ledge that ran along the bottom of a slope lit by silver highlights, which extended a hundred yards above me and ended in dark. I laid my pack on the ground, confident that this would be my only night out. My tongue was sandpaper. I pulled on the tube, removed the bladder from my pack and placed it on the ground. I pressed it with my palms to push fluid from the tube, but sand shone clear through the bladder and only air bubbles moved along inside.

I saw the tubes the minute I rushed into the maternity to give my wife the good news. They were attached to bags that hung from a metal stand above my exhausted wife's bed. Doctors had practically tied her to the bedposts for two weeks after they diagnosed her with preeclampsia. I had rushed in to tell her that a nurse had shown me the two-pound baby pulled from Nicole's body while she was unconscious. The nurse had told me, "She's tiny, but she's tough. I have to put her back," then carried the infant away on a yellow plastic tray, covered in blood.

Another nurse had appeared. "You can go see your wife now."

"Where is she?" The nurse pointed to a door. I walked in and faced a corridor. "Do you know where my wife is?" I asked the woman behind a glass wall with papers in her hand.

"Kaplan?" She pointed to a grey corridor with women in beds on each side. My wife was smiling. "Oh, thank God, that's over." She was entangled in tubes going in and out of her yellow smock. "Did you see the baby?"

"Yes, honey." The nurse's words came. "She's tiny but tough."

"Where is she? I haven't seen her," said Nicole.

"I don't know. Let me help you with the smock." I lifted her yellow garment but could not pull the tube through. I reached up with my other hand and took the intravenous device off the holder. Blood started to fill the plastic tube in my hand. The last thing I heard before falling to the floor was a nurse screaming, "Don't do that. Watch out."

When I woke, my wife was laughing — "You fixed that."

A nurse stood over me.

"Why don't you get up now."

I got up off the floor of the runnel, attached my headlamp to my forehead and explored the ledge. I saw a forty-foot-high barrier wall in front of me and scanned it with my light. It ran from one side of my glittering runnel across to the other. The left side had a lumpy surface with many small cracks; the right was smooth sandstone. A whirl of helicopters overhead interrupted. Their red and blue lights flashed. I pulled out my silver emergency blanket and rushed to place the reflective sheet on the smooth side of the rock wall. I stood on the sand, held the sheet down with one hand, leaned my forehead at an angle to the reflective blanket and, with my other hand, clicked the headlamp, flashing emergency signals at the sky for ten minutes or so.

"Nobody knows I'm missing." The place was dead silent. I heard engine hums and saw the outline of a passenger jet far above moving towards the moon. I smoothed the flimsy silver blanket again and made the emergency signal, a series of three quick flashes followed by a brief pause, repeating the pattern over and over again. No response. Just like the whirling helicopter blades with their colorful lights, the slim trunks of the humming planes were not in my world. I gathered the emergency blanket and walked ten yards back from the wall to my orange pack.

Another plane slid by along the same path, and I noticed it was tiny compared to the growing whiteness of the moon. I didn't rush back to the wall to try to signal it. I didn't really mind being in the little runnel. The sun that had hounded me on my long march was gone, and the moon had taken its place. The brighter the warm moon glowed, lighting the silver hills, the more comfortable the place became, and the more the little boy inside me lit up.

After Purple Canyon, the voice and smiling eyes of a young kid had grown inside me. It had replaced the tough guy who had met the challenge of jumps down the kaleidoscopic landscape and traversed the hill of thorns. The cowboy cholla playing cards at the rock warrens were the desert friends of this kid, and he had enjoyed whooshing down the smooth sandstone slide. Now this kid, who I later named "Sweet Eyed Boy," had found a nursery under the guardianship of his friend, the moon.

I laid my head on the black waistband of my pack and wrapped the silver emergency blanket around my body. I was comforted by the smile etched on the moon's face, and I turned away from the large rock barrier, which might be an obstacle in the morning. The bright blue and white stars of the Northern Cross rose alongside the moon; together they formed a cradle toy above me, a kite with a ball of yarn. Vega emanated cobalt blue. I fell asleep in Baby Canyon.

III.

Day two
Saturday, September 25

Ursula and Karl strolled through the
parking lot to start their morning walk.
Ursula saw that my car was not there.
"He's probably enjoying the desert," she said.

I WOKE IN the faint light of dawn. The sun was not
yet visible, but the moon was a white circle in the pale
blue sky. Gorgeous Vega and her companions Altair
and Deneb were gone. With the silver veins of earth
no longer glowing and the surrounding desert visible,
I saw cute little Baby Canyon for what it was — a slight
dip in an endless stretch of hills. I looked along my
elongated shadow to where I had entered this runnel
the night before and saw weathered grey and white
sandstone ridges extending below the moon. Turning
around to look in the direction I intended to take, I
saw that the forty-foot wall which blocked me was
surrounded by the very same sandstone formations,
and these extended above the wall and beyond to
where the steaming sun sat.

I had to get back my purple place of inner bliss,

which had become a marker on the map of memory, my only way out of the wilderness. I left my stuff lying on the ledge and stepped down to walk east into the sandstone hills, searching for a passage to circumnavigate the wall. After a fifteen-minute walk, I found myself in a dead-end, stretching my neck upwards at a steep hill six times my height. Anxious that I could not even see my runnel or my stuff from where I stood, I returned to the barrier exhausted, hungry, and thirsty. There was no access to the sandstone hills to the east of the barrier. I knew I had to go over it somehow. The left side looked like nature had decorated the surface with broken giant's teeth. The smooth right side had a faint bull's-eye of pink veins on its face. It was five times my height. I stretched my arms and rested my exasperated head against the cool smooth surface. Scratching the side of my head in wonder at how I had wandered into a place I couldn't get out of, I looked back and forth from faint bull's-eye to giant's teeth, then after repeated visualizations of my body tumbling and my head cracking against the ground, I postponed the climb.

My stuff was lying around on the flat sand where I had slept. I shoved the flimsy emergency blanket back into my pack. The drying lacerations on my arms and legs itched. I pulled my medical kit from my pack and zipped it open, looking for the lavender and white packets of antiseptic pads. The moisture of the pads felt as refreshing as an ocean swim, but they did nothing for my thirst — my coarse and itchy tongue like the small hand-held sanding pad in my garage, a thick rubber inside with harsh sandpaper outside.

The daytime moon waited silently at the entry to the little runnel and watched my search for the dates in my pack. Dried to my bones, the luscious black fruit offered a remedy. But my mouth would not let me chew it. The sweet date stuck like a lump to the roof of my mouth. I spit it onto the sandstone floor of Baby Canyon and threw the remaining dates as a possible signal to other hikers of the missing hiker I had become.

I pulled my collapsible cup from my pack and extended the white plastic sections. With it held in front of me, I opened my fly and watched an extremely dark, yellow urine fill the container. As I raised it to my lips, the stench hit my nose before the liquid reached my mouth. It got to my lips but not much further. I couldn't swallow, even with my nose held shut. I spit it out on the sand, saying to myself, "I'd rather be dead."

It might have been 8 a.m. on Saturday when I turned away from the splotch of date and urine on the canyon floor. The day had already driven the cool from the canyon. The sun was a time bomb on the horizon. I didn't need a thermometer to see which way the temperature was going. With the moon behind me, I returned to the wall.

The ragged rust-colored pile had some toeholds. Though I felt the kinship of the moon and the little boy inside me hadn't forgotten the comfort of Baby Canyon, I didn't want to stay there forever after making one wrong step and falling backwards, becoming a new lump at the foot of the pile. Just another of nature's mistakes, which is what the wall looked like. I crisscrossed the ground and searched the giant teeth-like obtrusions of the wall for a spot to stick my left foot into, so that then I could lean on my stick with my strong right shoulder to propel myself up. From that first step, I would scramble up and over. The words of my orthopedic surgeon rang in memory, "There is nothing we can do to repair your left shoulder. Your tear is deeper than your shoulder joint, in the armature beneath."

Surveying the perimeter, I walked back and forth across the tiny selvage, the broken stones in front of this fifteen-foot stretch of the wall. I was convinced the surgeon stood behind me on the sandy ledge in his white jacket, peering through his eyeglasses, watching my search for a giant's tooth to place my left foot upon. I spent more time walking the fifteen-foot stretch than the half-mile search for an alternative had taken, but found no safe launching step for my left foot. The low morning sun cast warning shadows past my legs. My urine had already dried in the sands behind me. There was a small ledge about four feet up the ragged patch of rocks that my strong right foot could reach, if only my weak left shoulder would allow me to use my left hand and lean on my stick a few seconds. After spending at least an hour looking for a way around and then surveying the wall over and over, I finally decided to go for it. I threw my pack on my shoulder, I leaned on the stick in my left hand, raised my left foot into the ledge, and threw my right foot uphill.

In the few seconds in the blue air between the sand and the toehold, as I leaned on my stick, terror filled my left shoulder. It felt like a surgeon's scream behind me would itself tear my left armature, I'd hear it rip, the stick would fly into the sky, and the last sound I'd hear would be my head banging on a rock. But the stick and shoulder held, and my right foot sailed into the crevice without my left shoulder cracking. I pulled my left leg up beside it. Then, kneeling into the face of the pile, I crawled up the wall like a four-legged spider and lifted my torso onto the other side with the stick in my fist.

The thin wafer of the daytime moon stayed behind me. The moon was my mother; she was my guide.

She was everything to me! With her on my shoulder, I reached the sheep bones, then the ghost lands of blowing talc. I found the enchanted purple rocks and walked through. But downhill from the apex, at the end of the canyon, several washes twirled across the basin all headed towards where I had come from the day before, in the direction of the warming sun. I turned to the moon for guidance. We picked the broadest arroyo, and I walked on.

Walking through the arroyo, which rose on a slight incline through heavy sand, cramped my calves. In some spots the path narrowed, and one was forced to squeeze between boulders, where diminutive hedgehog cactus hid beneath soft brattle bushes. When I brushed past the harmless flat leaves, I felt the tiny spines scratch my calves. But certain Joshua trees alongside familiar boulders were encouraging landmarks, affirming my hope that my selection would lead to the wide highway of the day before, and then I'd get back to the tire tracks.

But after a mile, the trail ended in a wall. It had seemed like his plan would work and the missing hiker would find his way back. He had found the blessed canyon, and then he needed only to needle his way through the winding arroyos and the land of glowing cholla to get to the turn-off by the truck tracks. He turned his worn body back to the moon.

The sun climbed behind me as I followed the moon back to where I stood an hour and a half earlier, the mouth of Purple Canyon. I stared at what the higher sun now made visible, a giant drainage system of which my magic canyon was but a tiny part. The moon hung over a slope that looked like cake batter in a mile-wide version of my mom's old mixer bowl. Scores of rivulets descended to the basin, with several headed away from the moon in the direction I needed.

I stood beneath a patch of white clouds at the foot of the canyon and stared at each of the trails winding down around me. Exhausted and warm in the rising heat, I had to choose one and only one. I would not have another chance. Any of these arroyos would keep the moon on my shoulder, but only one would lead to the tire tracks. When the sun's rays pierced the clouds and lit a path a few feet in front of me, I took it. The moon and I stepped along under the awning of puffy clouds, leaving the other trails at the canyon mouth.

I felt a strong tugging on my calves as I climbed higher on the chosen arroyo into a vista of soft brown desert hills. I saw little white puffs of cloud filled by the sun's angular morning rays also rising. The sand dunes ahead looked like baked marshmallows on sweet potato pie. Emotional boundaries disappeared. My mind shut completely. The tugging on my calves left. I was lifted along the trail. I was part of what I saw. It was part of me.

It was just this past Yom Kippur when, as usual, our congregation had enjoyed the annual visit of one of the founders of the Jewish Renewal Movement, Zalman Schechter Shalomi. He only came to our temple once a year. And each year, the bearded scholar sat in a high, padded chair by the stained-glass windows on the bema and asked if anyone had a question.

I raised my hand.

"Stephen Hawking says God is not necessary for the universe to exist."

The rabbi smiled and answered, "He could be right, but not if God is the universe."

In his mindless rise up the hillside, the lost hiker felt the unity, but his brief satori ended when his small footpath crested the hillside of roasted marshmallows and he faced a series of amber hills that extended beyond. He followed his little trail to where it ended abruptly in a pile of dunes, where countless trails circled inconclusively. He stood paralyzed in the puzzling junction. Ahead of him, the white torch in the sky threw rich blue shadows on the land. The moon had led him to an unreadable maze. His faithful friend was just another adornment in the land of the sun.

The pit of mingling trails was a barbeque, and I was the meat. Even a Bedouin would drop dead in the spot where I stood. Everything was a mass of white until I turned and saw a brown and green hillside. A sloppy surface of creosote bushes, gravel, sand, large rocks, and low tight bunch grass clung to a steep hill, and the miserable, forty-five-degree hillside had one remarkable feature: an isolated single needle pine with broad green branches stood midway up the hill.

A deep gulley filled with broken rocks snaked from my boots to just below the solitary pine. I had only to get there. I would not escape the desert, but I had to escape the heat. The flap of my hat protected my shoulders, but the mass of the sun was on my legs, back, and butt. Each time I lifted my legs in the dirt and rock trench, the weight of my boots resisted. I seemed slower with every step. At points along the way, the gulley was shoulder height, and I worried that I might not be able to pull myself out when I reached the evergreen, but I was lucky. Where the tree was, the trench was only a few feet high. I pulled myself out and collapsed in the dirt at the foot of the pine.

The single needle pine threw a lace pattern over my back. Downhill in the snaking gully, white-hot rocks glared. I took the limp bladder from my pack and placed it on the ground. I tried to suck water from the flat camelback. A sound came out. With a turn of the bottom seal, it emitted a pop. I stuck my fingers inside and licked off two solitary drops.

In the mustard-hued ridge across the canyon, I

heard people's voices. Behind the tree, the claps of imaginary horse's hoofs beckoned. I blew my orange whistle repeatedly. Three sharp high-pitched sounds, a silent interlude, then, three more whistles. But no people poked their heads over the ridge. No muscular black horse reared its handsome head.

Rising on an arc, the hot white sun burned a wide aurora out of the sky. Silica and other minerals in the gully lit up. Hundreds of gray rocks emanated reflections from their veins. My shoulders burned as the emissions of light and heat from the stones added to the feeling I was baking. My oasis of shadows pulled into the tree. The moon was a useless dot, watching the drama. The sun could be seen moving in a circle above the canyon, behind the tree, chasing me — a disheveled straw doll before it.

I moved closer to the trunk and feel asleep. The sun rose above Tree Canyon and turned southwest. The orange rim and silver edge of the disk peeked in above the lofting branches. I dove beneath the lower boughs, deeper into the cool shadows. As if I were mining the fir close to the trunk, I pulled rocks out and shoved my pack under the limbs, falling asleep the second my head rested on the padded black waistband. Only my bare legs stuck out from the shelter of my tree. The sun lit every stone in the canyon. My exhausted legs became the hands of an alarm clock, burning red to wake me each time the sun rose higher. This soft, green creature was everything to me as the relentless sun rose to its apex. Like a little boy lost in the neighborhood, I had found this adopted parent who suffered me burrowing inside it and breaking off pieces of its flesh. In a trance of thirst and exhaustion, I kept breaking branches, throwing aside stones, falling unconscious, was wakened, and shoved my padded pack deeper beneath the dangling green needles until I snuggled against the silver trunk.

IV.

Saturday Night

Our home message machine got a call
from Swiss Health Resort, saying I had
left Friday morning and hadn't returned.
My wife didn't pick up the message.

I WOKE LATE in the afternoon and came out from beneath the tree. In front of me, across the trench I had scrambled up, I saw a barren, hundreds-of-feet high, sandstone wall. I turned to look behind the tree. Splashes of short grass and green agave blades suggested life. My mother's voice filled the plaza on Avenue D when she opened the metal-framed window of the projects apartment and yelled, "Eddie, come get your milk and cookies." But the imagined sounds died, and I blew again into the lip of the whistle to emit the beep-beep-beep, but it brought nothing.

Neither of the canyon slopes was responsive. I could not climb on legs deadened by two days of walking. I looked up the narrow plateau to see what my prospects might be if, tomorrow, I continued uphill past the evergreen. But all I saw was another high ridge. Below me, the narrow trail snaked down around boulders and bunch grass to the floor of the basin. "This is some fucking celebration hike; I could be dead tomorrow." I tried to figure out the evening.

Tree Canyon compared unfavorably with Baby Canyon. I scanned the un-climbable cliffs for signs of life — the last of the sun's direct rays had left the canyon; the burnt orange wall had paled to yellow; a breeze blew through the exposed plateau, and the place was already cold.

The open area in front of the tree, about twenty feet by thirty, seemed like a good place to set up a fire ring of large stones within which I imagined lighting a large fire and then lying down and sleeping beside it to remedy the cold. I searched the large shrubs in my perimeter but there were no large stones. I looked in the twilight for firewood but found no large pieces, only a few twigs. I was in an alien environment, but I pushed that thought away from me, and with a few scraggly sticks in hand, I pulled a little metal tube of emergency matches from my pack, sat down on the ground in front of the small twig pile, and unscrewed the cap. With the cap unscrewed, the thick waterproof red heads came into view. They were not designed for the desert but for protection in a wet environment, and wouldn't light until scraped across the graphite striking surface several times. Finally, crouched down, I struck just right, the little burst whooshed, I inserted the flame in the pile, and the scraps caught; but when I stuck in more twigs, the fire expired.

After thirty-six hours without water, my mouth felt like the underside of a loaf of rye bread coated in corn flour. I scratched my tongue with my fingernails. I saw a yucca plant thirty yards down the plateau. It was like all the others I had seen yesterday and today, a dried-out circle of sharp green spears around a two-foot-high, grayish-brown trunk. But I was so fucking thirsty that I suddenly remembered something my friend Irena had told me when we had passed a flowering yucca on a springtime hike. Irena had pointed to the green bowl of spears circling the trunk of the plant and told me, "Look, there in the bottom, that is where you get water if you are stuck or lost in the wilderness."

I thought of the water in the yucca's trunk and gave up on fire making, pulled my Swiss Army knife from my waist pouch, and crossed the gravel plateau to the plant. I knew that the lingering sunlight might disappear at any moment, and I was so nervous at leaving the tree which had protected me that as I stepped over the ground to reach the yucca, I turned my head back to the evergreen every few yards, checking my orientation.

I sat down in front of the yucca and opened my

Swiss Army knife to its largest blade. The three-foot-high trunk of the plant was about one foot wide. I sat down cross-legged in front of it and saw that the base was sheathed in a hard bark of vertical gray strips. The plant was also protected by an array of spear-shaped stalks, each about three feet tall, circling the base in every direction. The points of the spears were very sharp and could easily pierce my skin, which was already lacerated from yesterday's scrapes and falls. The plant was designed to protect itself, including from lost hikers.

I slashed at the spear tips from a seated position, using the biggest Swiss Army knife blade, but there was not enough force from my arms to cut the thick stalks. I stood up to increase my leverage over the plant and held individual fronds in my left hand while slashing their tips with the right. This worked best with a smaller blade, and as I removed the tips of a couple of stalks, it seemed like I was getting closer to the water in the trunk. But when I pulled with both hands on the disarmed stems, they stuck to the base. None of the fronds budged, but I had been pulled closer to the defiant plant. I had to get a closer look at the base.

It was dusk on the plateau. The hillsides and shrubbery were losing coloring; all outlines were blurring. I turned from the yucca and again took a quick glance at my tree, checking that I had the same bearings towards it as earlier. Pivoting back to the yucca, I stuck my head in an opening between its stalks to see what gave them such holding power. It was that they wound inside each other at the trunk and were part of the hardened, thatched bark protecting the plant. The sky had darkened on the high plateau while I was working on the plant. The cliff walls on both sides of me disappeared. I had to postpone my attack on the yucca until dawn. I left the formidable plant and walked the sixty-degree angle across the plateau to my pack at the foot of the evergreen.

Sitting five feet in front of the cone-shaped tree, I took off my boots. Her green needles had turned blue as the exposed plateau of Tree Canyon chilled. I pulled out the tattered emergency blanket from my pack, then positioned the dirty orange bag with the black pad towards the tree. Lying back on the ground with my headlamp to my left and hiking stick to my right, I rested my neck on the pad. I pulled the emergency blanket around me. I shook the flimsy blanket out to its full length, pulled it over me, and tucked it in on both sides of my chin between my shoulders and the pad. I pulled my knees up and wrapped the bottom of the damaged metallic sheet around my feet. I heard it rip. I fidgeted around to cover my extremities. The full white moon and blue and white giants of the Northern Cross rose above the tree. Those cradle toys of the night before soothed me, and I fell asleep.

In a dream, I pulled the large red tarp in my trunk over me. Instead, a chill on my legs woke me, and I watched the large piece of the aluminum sheet that had covered my legs float away and snag itself on the bristles of a Joshua tree. Chills rode up my midsection, but I had no desire to chase the piece, headlamp or not. I sat up, pulled my emergency toilet paper from my pack, and shoved what was left of the blanket inside my shirt and shorts for insulation, wrapped toilet paper around my arms and legs, then fell asleep, a mummy like those little kids that were carried dead from Hilary's neonatology ward.

Late in the evening, Nicole picked up the message on our answering machine. She ran in to tell her guest Kathy, "Something horrible has happened. Ed never does anything like this. He's missing." She made a series of frantic phone calls to Swiss Health Resort and found out that Ursula and Karl had reported their suspicions to the Desert Hot Springs Police at 6 p.m.

Kathy stayed with Nicole in Los Angeles, postponing her return flight to Maine. They decided not to inform my family until they had more information.

An hour later, I woke up freezing, with toilet paper dangling off my limbs. Other pieces hung like flowers off bushes on my perimeter. Blue Deneb and its companion stars were gone. The entire plateau was lit in ghostly blue light reflecting off the dirt and plants. Even my evergreen, ten feet away, seemed off kilter and unbonded to me. With everything weirded out, I had to make sure that I hadn't lost the yucca. I scanned the plateau for tomorrow's source of desperately needed water, but saw only scraggly outlines of plants. Cold, I grabbed my pack, stepped to the tree, shoved it under the lower branches and crawled in on top, hoping for a repeat of the restful daytime naps.

I wanted to fall asleep facedown on the black pad but couldn't, so I turned and saw through the stiff limbs a menacing moon. It flooded the canyon with un-friendly light. And more than the moon had turned against me. The tree also. The green bounce and vibrancy of midday were gone; the gray branches hovered like dead limbs. I shifted the pack closer to the trunk and slid beneath the branches, adjusting the ragged toilet paper on my arms and legs. I was close up against her but emotionally distant. The helpful plant had turned heartless. I could not fall asleep again. I slid out on the eerie blue dirt, with pieces of silver sheet and toilet paper attached, and sat up.

Friendly or not, the tree was all I had. I sat in the silver-blue dark near her skirts. I could not leave to fetch anything that wasn't close. The silver shreds of blanket in the Joshua tree ten feet to the side of the evergreen might as well have been two miles away. I pulled the remaining attached remnants of the blanket tight around me for warmth, but I was still cold. I remembered the white container and pulled out the emergency matches once more. I built a tiny pyramid of twigs and, sitting in the dark, struck matches repeatedly on the black graphite container top. Finally one lit, and a white burst of light threw the match's shadows over my palm. I placed the flame under the twigs. But they did not ignite. Again and again, I repeated the cycle of making several strikes on the striking pad before a match lit, placing it under the twigs, blowing frantically, and watching as each went out. Finally, I got orange flames to grow inside a small pyramid of twigs. But then they died.

I sat there. I thought of how I hated wool Cub Scout outfits so much that I never moved on to Boy Scouts. I remembered my brother Joe and my father walking out the door of our apartment with packs on, early on a weekend morning, carrying sleeping bags and camping equipment. The closest I had gotten to any of that was in a picture of a Boy Scout's ceremony in a family album. In the photo, my brother Joe got his Eagle badge as Dad, the scoutmaster, smiled on the podium. The group photo included Mom and me.

My mouth felt like a sand trap but with no hope

of cutting the yucca until morning, I turned to my other problem. Lacerations had turned my arms and legs into a pattern of red fishnet stockings on white skin. I flicked on the headlamp. With the narrow band of light beside me, I took out the second violet and white packet of medical cream and soothed my arms and legs.

The light beam pointed to the inner thigh of my left leg, as if it were my nurse from ten years earlier standing over my bed after quadruple bypass surgery. "They had to take a vein to replace your clogged artery. Put this red antiseptic on twice a day." Sitting in the dark with the beam shining on the faint scar reminded me how I'd been kept in the dark on the big deal that had led to the heart attack. My partner and I were standing by our desks slapping high-fives when I had picked up my desk phone to call the escrow company and asked, "When will my check be ready?"

The answer, "Oh, didn't the buyer and seller tell you?"

"Tell me what?"

"The seller gave the deposit back to the buyer."

"Why didn't you tell us?" I had asked.

"Oh, they said not to mention it and that they would tell you."

I had a lot of bills to pay and was pissed off. I could not stop thinking about how fucked up it was that the clients had cancelled the deal without telling me. I took an extra-long hike the next day, but it didn't relax me. Instead, I got excruciating cramps, so bad that I couldn't move my legs. The hike ended with me stuck on a local trail in the afternoon sun. After being pulled to the shade by a helpful hiker, I went to the hospital. Half unconscious, I overheard the angiogram technician say, "This guy should be dead."

I made a promise to myself after quadruple bypass surgery that I'd never get worked up like that again. Now, I took the small tube of gooey red from inside the medical kit and gently rubbed it into the faint scar. I medicated and bandaged my worst lacerations, then slathered the gooey red liquid all over my arms and legs and waited for the sun to rise.

V.

Day three
Sunday, September 26

As LIGHT FILLED Tree Canyon, I walked over to the yucca and stood in front of her. One by one, I held the stems of the yucca in my left hand and cut off their tips with my right. I still had trouble. The big blade of the knife got stuck halfway through the strongest stems, so I switched to the small blade. This worked. The place got hot as I cut the tips off enough blades in one area to get to the dark grey trunk. I stuck the tip of the knife in and saw soft pistachio inner bark around the blade just six inches from my face. It looked moist. I wanted to cut a slot, but the blade that I had stuck into the trunk could not cut downward. I pulled it out, opened my knife to all the different blades attached, and saw the fish-cleaning blade. I shoved in the point and sawed a vertical slot, anticipating a drink. The cut looked like it was filled with water. Something glistened across the cut's little lips, but when I put my mouth to it and sucked, nothing came out.

The trunk had water but held it in its skin. I could see it but not taste it. I was tired of standing and sat down. I decided to pull off stems, hoping soft ends attached to the trunk would be moist. But the yucca was tougher and smarter than I was. When I pulled at a stalk with my arms, it didn't budge, and instead my butt slid on the sand closer to the trunk. In response, I took a systematic approach to frond removal. First, I cut the tip of the stalk off with the small blade, then removed its supporting thatching on the trunk with the large and saw blades, then clamped the tiny pliers of the knife on the stem, tight in my fist, and pulled. The results were nothing to brag about. Sticking my arm out to grab one, I imagined reaching into the veggie drawers of our refrigerator at home for a cold stick of celery and hearing the plump green stalk crunch. No such luck. Each was disappointing in a different way. Some, bone dry, tasted like paper on my tongue. Others had small amounts of moisture. I sat cutting, de-barking, and pulling stalks until my arms flopped to my sides.

After three hours' labor, I had eight or nine un-chewed stalks lying at my feet. The sun had lit up the canyon; it was time to leave. Even if I could hide under the tree all day, I could not take another cold night. I sat by the yucca and looked around Tree Canyon. Many green and yellow shrubs were lit in soft light. I wished I were a Native Mojave who could understand which of the plants held food or water.

But the knowledge was hidden from me.

I shoved the stalks into my pack to suck on later. I smiled at the yucca that had withheld its water and tipped my hat to it. High walls still blocked my exit on three sides — the shear wall of sandstone across from the evergreen, the ragged wall of rocks and shrubs behind it, and the steep, thin, neck of the canyon beyond the tree, blocked by thick shrubbery. I had to go back down to where I had come from in order to find a safe place, sheltered from both daytime sun and nighttime cold. I peered anxiously at the endless tan maze of rocky humps and dry riverbeds below me. A pale sun was low in the sky over my left shoulder, just above the eastern wall of the plateau behind the tree, beginning its daily journey westward. I lowered myself into the gully.

I stepped around the boulders and rocks that had lit up the place the day before when the sun was high, and I hid under the tree. They were covered in the shade of the hillside and were ordinary grey and white obstacles in the dirt track. In a few minutes, I reached the maze of sandy humps that had looked like blue dunes beneath the high sun of the day before. Now in the gentle light, I could see they were dirty white mounds of sand and small rocks. A series of runnels and ditches wound around and through. The dead ends of some were visible but others seemed to go on and on, making them possible trails. I remembered that I had made sort of a U-turn the day before when I had come from the lower basin. I had to go back in that direction, since God only knows what I might find higher up, so I took one path that curved back around behind me.

As I followed the curve of the trail, gravity made it easy to stroll through the powdery passages, and I told myself, "These must have been the marshmallow hills from yesterday." The rising sun was now behind me, throwing my shadow ahead. The daytime full moon was up in the pale blue sky in front of me. I no longer needed to find any landmark or navigable feature, only a safe place to stay. After a twenty-minute walk, my boot almost stepped on something that made no sense at all — my plastic bag with dates inside! I couldn't begin to contemplate the why and wherefore of it, but again the desert had surprised me.

The dates marked a spot I'd left twenty-four hours earlier, and it was much hotter than when I had left. My thirst had taken over, and I stared through the plastic bag at the cracked fruit like a visitor from a planet with an entirely different cuisine, my mouth too dry to even want to taste them. I was an empty body standing there. I looked behind me at the uneven wall of giant teeth I had struggled to climb a day before, puzzled that I had come down without noticing it, and baffled that I'd found myself on the same sandy landing. But the wall, the landing, and the dates were all separate visuals to me, not part of a place called Baby Canyon. My shadow pointed in the direction of the moon, on the lip of a sandstone ridge ahead. I followed the hard, bleached road up and over.

At the crest, the path entered a narrow road with large walls on both sides. Big columns of talus, portions of the eroding sandstone sticking out from the canyon walls, reminded me that I was back on the road-like arroyo which went all the way back to Purple Canyon. I knew I could not make it there or even as far as the glowing cowboy cholla. I only needed a safe place to stay where someone might find me. I walked around a ten-foot tall boulder that had fallen and landed in the middle of the channel due to erosion or some extreme weather event. As bad as my luck was, at least I was not walking below that wall in a flash flood.

My phone and its clock were dead, but it must have been 10 a.m. when I circled that boulder. A minute later the heat on my shoulders became unbearable, and I felt like I was carrying the sun. The walls were white hot. The road was white hot. I had to hide somewhere. Fifty yards ahead, a coral-colored rock stood out from the whiteness. It looked like a man-sized clamshell. I reached it in the heat and saw that it was tilted away from the hot sun at a thirty-degree angle. There was room inside its black shadow for me. I got inside feet first beneath the rock and, pulling my knees up into my groin, dragged my pack along with me, positioned the black pad snug as possible against my neck, and fell asleep in the wonderful cool space.

I woke what must've been every few minutes to check the shadow, sticking my head out from under the rock, craning my neck back towards where I had come from. Each time I woke from a few minutes sleep, I saw that the sun was higher and the shadow had shrunk. It was hotter than Saturday. When the heat poured in, my safe haven would turn into a frying pan.

There was nowhere to escape. On either side of me, runoff debris roasted at the bottom of steep cliff walls. I couldn't make it back to Tree Canyon even if I wanted to or go very far in the heat. Wherever it was would have to be ahead. I took a few seconds of my awakenings between naps, when I wasn't fretting over the sun and the shadow, to look out over the sand through the open side of the rock for a place to hide. In one of those waking seconds, I saw a separate rock formation in a bend on the road, about fifty yards ahead. It was an angular rock wall maybe twenty feet high, tipped liked a roof over the ground below. I closed my eyes and fell asleep again, but each time I woke, I squinted for an opening in that wall. In one waking moment, I thought I saw one. The slit in the wall, if it was there, looked like it could save me. I might be able to move through the opening.

I hoped I was right. I hoped that it led to a sheltered canyon. I didn't have three search engines checking for hotel rooms out there. I fell asleep once more and woke when it felt like someone had stuck a heat lamp in my face. I saw the bottom half of the glowing light just under the lid of my rock. I got out from under the clamshell and limped across fifty yards of scrub grass, dragging my pack behind me. As I got closer to the cracked walls, the opening became visible. I slipped through.

I was inside what I had seen from under the rock and was so thankful. I could tell immediately that it was a safe place. The three-sided rock outcrop, about fifty yards square with walls twenty feet high on two sides, was my salvation. A ten-foot tall acacia stood in the center, its red bark and green leaves stood out from the ground of small grey stones and sand. I limped into the patch of shade the cat claw leaves threw off and sat down. Out of the sun's clutches, my mind shifted to my scratchy throat, which felt like it was tightening inside itself. I remembered the choice yucca stalks from Tree Canyon that I had stuffed in my pack that morning. My orange pack was beside me on the sands, and I opened it up and pulled out the stems. The heat of my morning search had dried them to pointed brown crisps. Exasperated, I tossed the burnt stalks to the ground, put my head on the pack, and fell asleep.

I was back at my desk and pushing papers around. I couldn't find the document I needed. Remembering it was in the file cabinet behind me, I leaned on the desk to get up. But I was unable to stand. Opening my eyes, I saw my hand on sandy gravel. I was facing a rocky wall. I remembered where I was. The shadow of the acacia had pulled back, and the canyon was a radiator. The sun burned. I couldn't stand, I reached for my hiking stick, propped myself up, grabbed my orange pack, dragged it twenty feet, and shoved it into a black stripe of shade along the cliff wall. I lay down with my neck on the black waist pad and feel asleep.

VI.

Sunday Afternoon

A SENIOR CITIZEN *staying at the campground noticed that the day hiker who'd parked nearby on Friday had not returned, and he became concerned. He flagged down a Park Ranger's car, and the ranger, Melanie Lloyd, informed Dan Messaros, the head of the Park Rangers' criminal investigations unit. Melanie notified my wife that my car had been found and that it was in Black Rock Canyon Campground. According to witnesses, I had left it there on Friday afternoon and had not returned. Rangers asked for a picture of me to be e-mailed so they could post it on bulletin boards in Black Rock Canyon.*

Ms. Lloyd sought Nicole's help to begin an extensive series of interviews with anyone who might know my habits and whereabouts. Melanie also requested phone numbers of hiking buddies. She needed proof of ownership of my car and approval to search it in order to determine whether I had been a victim of foul play or in order to find a clue to my destination, such as a map. From pings on my phone, rangers would contact the last people I had spoken to, in case I might have told them where I was.

Ranger Jeffrey Ohlfs was Incident Commander in charge of the rescue effort. He authorized a "hasty search" of the area by members of his staff and all the trails in Black Rock Canyon to be closed so that his people could comb the pathways issuing from the parking lot.

At a large table downtown, men were arguing about money. It was late afternoon. I wanted to change my seat because sunlight was hitting my face over the shoulder of the guy in front of me. There were no seats available on the other side of the table. "This owner is too cheap to put in blinds." The sunlight got brighter and hotter. I squirmed around in my chair and rubbed my shoulder against a rough surface. I woke up in pebbled sand against a rock cliff, with my chest and shoulders covered by a merciful black shade. I would have gladly returned to the table. The canyon was lit by mid-day sun, the grey ground was white hot, and a wall of amber stone shone at me from forty yards away. My boots were five yards from me, spread apart, turned over on their laces. They sat on small runnels in the sand a few inches deep, tiny tracks of my sliding feet.

The sky weighed on my chest, but I struggled to my elbows and searched for my place in the landscape. I'd been dragging myself along, chasing the shade. I remembered the empty miles of scorched landscape dotted with black pebbles, blackened creosote plants, and yellowed scrub grass surrounding me. The sun had moved the cliff's shadow. I shoved my orange pack behind me and grabbed my stick. Without lifting my body, I pushed against the stick, and slid into the shifted shadow as my eyelids closed. In the projects on the Lower East Side, my dad was lying on the couch, and light came through the window. I was happy to see him there because he usually wasn't around. It was warm, and he didn't need a cover. A breeze from the East River moved the curtains. His bald head was on the pillow. His big hairy chest moved up and down. He looked like a happy bear. I had never seen him like that. I decided to leave the couch I was on and lie down next to him.

I walked over and lay down alongside him. He was much bigger than me, and I didn't take up much room. I fit into the space away from the window, and he was on the rest of the couch, closer to the breeze. My legs only went to his waist. He kept sleeping. I looked over his chest out the window and saw the daylight. The room was cozy. I started to fall asleep. His snoring did not bother me.

As I was falling asleep, I moved closer, resting on his arm and putting my head on his hairy chest. Just above the rim of his T-shirt. He jostled around and without opening his eyes said, "Get out of here." He

ED ROSENTHAL

lifted me in the arm I was on and threw me in the air. As I sailed across the room, I knew he didn't care where I landed.

I woke in the canyon. The white heat was gone. I tried to get up but my right leg buckled, so I held my stick and pushed down, using my left leg to stand, dragging my right alongside. Limping, but grateful that I had not lost my legs on an open arroyo, I went in my stocking feet to a flat rock twenty yards away in the middle of the enclosure and sat on the two-foot-high perch. From there, I could see the wide basin. Again I surveyed my situation. I'd be found one day, dead or alive. Out of the elements I could survive several days. My phone was long dead. The clip of a ballpoint hung on the pocket of my short sleeve shirt. I searched for paper in my pack. I took off my hat and tested my pen on the inner lid, and it worked, so I began a letter to my wife and daughter.

"Dear Hilary and Nicole, I love both of you not sure if I can make it out of here. I made a wrong turn and didn't take enough water. Call Andrew for my commission. Collect the life insurance."

Encouraged by my ability to communicate, I expanded my instructions: "Give my love to Gary, Jerry, Jeff, John Kaji, Harold, Mark Moniz, Tyson, Rabbi Debra, My Brother, Sister, Chris Cooney, Steven, and Felisa."

Writing the names of my friends, I felt better. As each name brought a different memory, my mind separated from the loneliness of my body on the rock. Many of my friends never had met each other, and I began to plan. "My funeral will be a wake. Have the Downtown poet Richard McDowell recite a poem."

Now, I became encouraged there might be a tomorrow. With the nylon hat turned over, the inside lid was perfect to setup a calendar chart. I put some straight lines across the inside of the rim and listed what had happened so far, leaving spaces for future days. On the top line:

"Friday, I got lost in the wilderness and slept in a cute little canyon. Saturday, couldn't get back and slept under a fir tree. Sunday, I found this place."

A horsefly sat watching as I wrote. He had found me under the clamshell rock and followed me across the fifty yards to this outcrop. He had attached himself to my shoulder beneath the acacia. Each time I dragged my body into the shadow during the long afternoon, he lifted off my chest a few inches, buzzed a small loop in the air and landed again on my chest. When I had gotten up from my last dream, he followed me over to the flat rock and sat there while I wrote messages to my wife and daughter. Most flies I would brush off, but I didn't feel like flicking my wrist at this one.

I lifted my pen and clicked the release. The point

withdrew. I placed the pen in my shirt pocket and stared at the fly sitting next to me. I'd come back to my friends later. The sky changed again. The sun disappeared behind the sheltering walls. I put the hat on my head and leaned on my stick to lift myself off the rock. My companion took off and stayed in the air behind me. My legs buckled worse than before.

Mom stood between my brother Joe and me, with her cane supporting her. We were on the wooden piers, the place where trawlers brought in their hauls. The black wall of a ship with slimy seaweed that stuck in the wooden planks of its bow slid in as sailors threw ropes down to tie to the posts. The East River was green and choppy. The place smelled like salt and rotten fish. We were above the boarded stalls where Mom bought the whitefish and pike that Russian Jews used to make gefilte fish.

We turned away from the boat and went across the pier. My brother held one of Mom's hands while she moved her cane with the other. When we turned sharp left onto a slippery gangplank to the fishmonger stalls, I heard her scream and saw her lose the grip of my brother's hand. Her black coat lifted, and her bad leg buckled out from under her. In a few seconds, she'd slid ten feet below us down the ramp.

"I can't get up. Go get somebody," she told my brother. I was so afraid for her. I walked down the incline and sat next to her and repeated, "Are you okay, Mommy?" People streamed from the stalls carrying fish wrapped in newspaper past us. I explained to them, "My Mom fell. My brother went to get somebody." A lady turned her head, made a sad face, and said, "Someone will be here soon," but then she walked away, up the slippery plank, like the rest of the people. I sat a long time with the river gurgling around the posts below me. My brother returned with a strong man in a navy-blue pea jacket. He lifted my Mom, carried her back to the street, and hailed a cab.

I stuck my ear inside the door jamb of my parent's room that night when the doctor came. He told Dad, "Your wife doesn't listen too easy. She has to give up that cane before something worse happens. We have to get her fitted for a full metal brace. You tell her what I said."

By the time we moved to Rockaway Beach, she was used to the steel and leather brace. Every summer day, she loaded her shopping cart with drinks and sandwiches and took my brother Joe, my sister Ann, and me a mile to the beach. She leaned against the cart and dragged her braced leg behind. We passed ten six-story red brick buildings, with children who might look out the window. Their mothers didn't limp and bob all over the place.

We rolled by the busted up, bleached bungalows

lining the last blocks to the beach. This stretch of relics from Rockaway's glory days was filled with broken glass. Skirting around the worst patches, we would reach the boardwalk. She grabbed the rusty railing and pulled herself up the steps to the long wooden planks.

Another set of stairs descended to the beach. She threw off her brace and beach dress. She dragged her weak leg to the water's edge. Free of land, she dove in under the green foam. She found the strong ropes and propelled herself along the string of orange barrels. The skirt of her black suit filled with ocean and bounced like a whale in the water.

Now, I dragged my leg through the sand to the wall. The fly followed behind. I pulled my pack from the wall to the foot of the acacia, positioning the black pad to face the moon. With my stick beside me, I lay down and watched the moon grow and light the floor of my last refuge. The blur of the fly buzzed, scouting the circumference of the tree. Then, absolute silence. The cliffs protected the place from wind but also blocked any view to either side of me.

Ahead, I saw faint red and amber lights of a desert community a few miles away. I could not move my legs to reach them. The blue star Vega came up to meet the ever-present moon over the canyon. The white giant Altair flashed alongside. The cradle toy of a diamond pendant and a white ball was back. I had found a protected alcove in the great basin. The walls shut out everything but the distant lights, the giant cross, and my friend the moon.

The fly settled down on the pack. We fell asleep.

VII.

Day four
Monday, September 27

I THINK ORION woke me. The constellation stood in the grey sky with the full moon over his shoulder. In winter evenings, in my backyard in Los Angeles, he looked like a warrior, holding his club with swagger, ready to protect the Seven Sisters from The Bear. But in Salvation Canyon, the club around his belt looked like a thermometer. He was a nursemaid with a blanket in the morning chill.

I sat up, grabbed my orange pack and pulled it around to my lap. The red and green medical kit was close to the top, its colors brilliant in the drab canyon. I opened the kit and pulled out my moisturizer. The damp gauze of the pad felt great on my arms and legs. My thirst was gone. I had no urge to scratch my mouth. I didn't feel like my tongue had a sand cover. I had stopped thinking about the red and blue water bottles in my trunk. I had stopped looking for little round pebbles in the sand to suck on.

Joshua Tree rangers called in volunteers to broaden the search. A central command post was set up in the main parking lot. The rangers found a partial footprint by my car door. They made copies and handed them out to the volunteers. They also duplicated the photo of me that Nicole had sent and posted copies on the central visitors' board.

Ranger Dan Messaros collected all the information he could to help direct the search. He contacted Jeff Wallace, my main hiking buddy, to learn what he could about my hiking abilities. Jeff told Dan, "That boy never gets tired. We hiked Whitney, Mt. Baldy, and Baden Powell together, and he was never worn out." There wasn't much to go on, but searchers were sent in groups to explore all the trails issuing from the parking lot where I had last been seen.

In the cool morning, I sat near the red trunk of the acacia beneath the green cat claw leaves and went through my pack. I found the two six-inch-long pieces of compressed fuel in a plastic bag at the bottom and took one out. I pushed my pack away, propped myself up on my hiking stick, stuck a fire starter on an angle in the sand next to the Acacia's trunk, and struck a match.

The match lit, and the starter caught. I backed away on my hands and knees. The middle section of the trunk bent behind the flames. But the brief eruption didn't grow. The tree's mid-section turned grey and smoldered. The limbs were untouched; the green leaves remained intact. The poorly lit signal fizzled out, leaving a pool of black resin on the ground.

I lifted the orange whistle to my mouth and frantically blew emergency signals. No one appeared. The day had no cloud cover. It was a searing replica of Sunday. The sun was barely off the ground, but the heat was already building. I leaned on my stick and followed Sunday's tracks into the shadow of the south wall. Everything was of a piece: the sun, the canyon walls, me, and the fly, who moved his grey wings to flutter in his own little circuit, then settled on my chest when I rested on my pack.

At noon, the volunteers returned to camp for lunch. They reported that they had found nothing. Ranger Ohlfs reached out to neighboring counties for more help. He called tracker Sheriff Jeff Joling of San Bernadino to broaden the search. Head Ranger Judy Bartzatt met with the sheriff in Joshua Tree Park to review.

On a green bench at the projects in front of the brick community center, all the teenagers were hanging out. Steve Salomon was prancing in front of the bench, his black raincoat fanned out behind him, doing a "Tail Feather." He was trying to look cool, like he was black. But he didn't. Holding his raincoat tail behind, he waved his umbrella in front and alongside. The tip came off and flew into Sarah Simon's eye.

Kids got up to run for help, but I wasn't surprised

when I couldn't and found myself in the familiar canyon, in a black mood, staring at the pool of resin beneath the acacia. It was around five o'clock. The heat had left the canyon. I dragged my pack to the scarred bush. The black resin had dried and encrusted the sand. It looked like I felt. The moon was sympathetic. It was over the western lip of the outcrop, in the direction of that unknown community lit by the lights of the night before. I stared at the moon and the mystery community, saddened by the reawakened memory of Sarah, who had died before the ambulance reached the hospital.

On my paper route, I rode my overloaded bike by a pretty girl I'd never met. "What's your name?" I'd shouted. The girl had smiled and waved hello. But one of her friends told her that my nickname was Rat, so whenever I approached her on my route or at the community center, she hid among her girlfriends. One day, Sarah told her I was a good match and things changed. Maxine and I went steady and eventually married.

Sitting there, remembering events from the projects fifty years earlier, I looked towards the desert community and wished that I had the strength to walk across what looked like several miles to reach it. But that was impossible on my weakened legs. I had a much more modest hope to make it to the only dense vegetation in the canyon, the array of weeds which stood by the northern wall. The weeds, whose stems had seemed translucent and their flounces white torches in the midday sun, now, in the late afternoon, were tan and pistachio-colored. They were thirty yards past the flat rock. If I could get to them and light my last fire starter, I'd raise a large signal that might be seen.

But my legs didn't have the stamina to cross the twenty yards of crushed grey pebbles to the flat rock and then the thirty yards of bunchgrasses to the wall. The total of fifty yards looked like miles, and I wasn't strong enough to hold a crouched position and light the flames I needed.

I stared at the weeds as I pulled my filthy pack to my lap with the back turned upwards and set the straps aside for a writing surface. I took off my hat and looked for a clear space. I unsnapped the life-saving neck protector extension and placed it on the bumpy surface. Pressing pen point into the nylon, I continued yesterday's funeral instructions.

"Throw my ashes onto Musch Trail in Topanga Canyon. Everyone is to get stoned and drunk and have Persian food with charbroiled tomatoes."

I watched as if through binoculars as Victor, my former boss and Mark, my best client, grabbed the handles of the food chest with my urn inside. They led a line of my friends and family from the shade of the giant oaks of the parking lot onto the sunny access road over Topanga Creek. Wolf carried a red and white bag of charcoal under his arm and Zoraster, a bottle of bourbon.

With the sun descended behind the southern wall, the weeds threw no shadows. The colors of the flounces faded to grey. The northern wall lost its sheen. I wanted to believe that I might make it across now, in the cooler canyon; I tried to lift my thighs off the rock, but the bones in my legs felt like they could not even raise me. I relaxed my hamstrings into the flat surface, shifted around, and gazed at my hat.

My friends reached the low wooden bridge over the small arm of the creek. Jeff pointed to the grove of pink mariposa. "See those flowers with bright orange insides, damned if he didn't point to those, every single time."

The moon brightened over the western lip of the canyon. It had turned into a broiled tomato. Its charcoal stripes were prison bars that locked the top of the canyon. I sat with my hat on my lap. I buttoned the top button on my shirt and stuffed the hem into my shorts. I had to do something. I couldn't reach the weeds to start a signal.

The wake followed the winding dirt road to the low wooden posts of the upper campground. Victor and Mark put the large metal chests down on a picnic table. Zoraster put his bottle beside. They crowded into a circle around a solitary pink lily growing at the edge of the camp. Jeff took out the silver urn. Richard recited the poem "I am a poor boy from the country." Jeff opened the urn, and with Hilary and Nicole at his sides, he threw the ashes over the lily, "Goodbye, buddy."

It must have been close to 7:30 p.m. when I knelt in the sand and arranged my boots, headlamp, and stick in a ring alongside the resin pool. The moon lit the top of the flat rock, but the scrub grass around it was splotchy with patches of dark. Beyond the splotches, the dark green skeletons of weeds. I needed to light a fire, but I couldn't be sure of my steps even if I had the energy.

They walked to the table. Wolf unzipped the bag of charcoal and shouted: "Let's cook up the whitefish and broiled tomatoes."

Zoraster lifted his bottle, "This is my best Bourbon." He passed it around.

I picked up my pen from beside me on the rock.

Irena grabbed the bottle. "He was crazy. He once took my car and left me stranded at an industrial property. We were so glad when he met Nicole and they had Hilary. Jesus Christ, what a character."

Seeing them pass the bottle around the table made

me feel better. But my wife and daughter looked mournful. I filled in the Monday section on my hat's chart. "Slept in the same spots as Sunday." I started a space for the Tuesday section, but I wasn't sure I'd make it to morning. I placed my pen back in the pocket of my sandy white shirt. I shoved my pack inside my circle of possessions.

After four dehydrated days on the Mojave, the sight of Blue Vega and giant Altair rising above the canyon had no pizzazz. I bent like an empty can by the scarred trunk of the acacia and recited the prayer for Jews who may not live until dawn.

Shema Yisrael Adonai Eloheinu Adonai Ekhad. Hear O Israel: the Lord is our God, the Lord is One.

A wispy funnel of clouds around me. Everything inside and outside was black and pervaded with illuminated objects, a gigantic Chumash sky painting. I floated upward inside with my hands extended towards the top. The white funnel was also moving as it stretched to the top of the black sky. But I was moving faster than the funnel itself. I was accelerating towards the extremely bright aperture at the very top. Effortless, accelerating bliss. I was eager to reach whatever was generating the brightness at the opening above.

A spectator, I was almost entering the light when an open palm with white cuffs on a black sleeve appeared. It blocked the opening. The bearded face of Moshe Greenwald, the young Chabad rabbi of Downtown Los Angeles, appeared. He smiled, then asked with his palm still held out, "Ed, are you really ready for this?"

I answered, "No" and woke up inside my body, on my pack alongside the half-burned acacia in Salvation Canyon. I was beneath a violet sky, the gown of a beautiful woman who wore an immense blue sapphire, a jeweled pendant reflecting off the black puddle of resin. I fell asleep, again.

Monday early evening, volunteers from the local Joshua Tree Search and Rescue reported results back to Rangers Messaros and Ohlfs. They had found no trace of "the victim." The vastness of the southwest desert required various groups to cooperate. Sheriff Joling sent a request out to a number of volunteer groups in the area for them to free up their schedules and rendezvous in the morning.

VIII.

Day five
Tuesday, September 28

TUESDAY MORNING, I lifted my head to check for the fly. He seemed to be sleeping still.

Members of the following teams were on scene at the search: Bear Valley SAR, San Bernardino Mountain SAR, Morongo Basin SAR, Morongo Basin Mounted SAR, Rim SAR, Wrightwood Phelan SAR, and San Gorgonio SAR Cave & Technical Rescue Team.

Sheriff Joling got to the planning meeting first. Volunteers started to trickle in, each equipped with twenty-four-hour supply packs. The sheriff related, "This would be the guy's fifth day in the sun. Only God could keep someone alive out there. We had people from throughout San Bernardino County — people on horseback, ground troops, and dogs."

Every search and rescue member was given a topographic map and a search plan to follow. Each searcher carried a GPS that fed onto a map in a central station and duplicated the coordinates of the area surveyed.

The map covered an area of about fifty-five square miles of desert wilderness. Colored ink lines on the printout showed where the searchers had been each day. The map the searchers received Tuesday had two colors only. Day One (Sunday) had a thick orange line that circled a very small area close to the top of the map, where it said Black Rock Canyon. Day Two (Monday) was red. The red markings covered an area three times the size of the orange, but still within the Black Rock Canyon quadrants.

The largest group of volunteers was Morongo Basin Search and Rescue, whose members were aware that the lost hiker was sixty-four years old. The photographer Robert Mohler, who documented their search through loose stones and inclines close to Warren View, was concerned. "We heard the guy had been out there five days in the heat. At his age, he couldn't have much left."

I was comfortable in the cool morning sands and just wanted to hang out by the acacia before applying my lotion. But when I went to sit up, my back muscles didn't support me. I threw my pack half on, grabbed my stick, and dragged myself from the blackened acacia to the cliff walls for support. The fly launched himself off my wrist to accompany me on the journey. We passed my empty boots, dampened by the night air, and two days worth of pockmarks I had left in the sand. My knees dragged the surface. The only sounds in the canyon, my grunts and the nick of the stick on a large pebble. When I reached the wall, I shoved the filthy orange pack in and leaned against the gray cliff; the fly landed his tiny legs on my wrist.

He then lifted two vertical feet into the air of the canyon above the nearby sands and suspended himself in space. He fluttered around as I opened the little pack of cream and pulled out the lotion-infused paper, then he lowered a foot to hover on rapid wing movements, steady above my left hand. His skeletal frame like a trick yoyo. As I sat and rubbed my filthy arms and legs with my right hand, dabbing the dried scabs of the wounds, I admired the blur of his miniature wings; in the dry air, against the canyon cliffs, he was intent on motionlessness. When I finished dabbing myself, my skinny friend descended in a straight vertical line, like a wiry helicopter, and landed where he liked to hang out, the bottom crease of my forearm.

The morning sky was not crystal clear. There was a girdle of cumulus clouds around Orion. The atmosphere was changing. The hairs on my legs were a bit moist. Orion's thermometer was not visible below his waist. I sat facing him, the fly on my shoulder.

I was across from Donny as a group of us played a game of "touch" on the black asphalt. We were in natural teams of scholastics versus tough guys. I was a scholastic. The girls sat on the wood bench by the side fence, watching. They were fascinated by Donny. They thought he was gorgeous but kept their distance because he was volatile. He was my assignment on the play, wiry but ten pounds lighter. Allen, our quarterback, raised his arm to fake a pass, and Donny tried to reach him. I lowered my shoulder to his ribs and shoved him against the grey mesh fence. Allen ran through the white goal line to score. Donny's pompadour flopped. He pulled out his comb and touched it up.

I felt for the crook of my neck and found the pack crumpled behind it against the wall. I pulled it out and placed it on the ground alongside me, pushing it along the wall with the black waistband face-up. I reached for the stick, pulled it close to me, and watched the shadow of the acacia. The natural clock was still in its morning position. I checked again for the tiny skeleton of the fly and closed my eyes.

I had shoved Donny into the mesh, just as a nicely dressed boy strolled by. He carried a beautiful mahogany brief case with a brass handle. It was Alan, on his way to a private school in Manhattan. I pointed my index finger towards him and said, "Hey Donny! That kid said you're a moron." Donny ran down the sideline, past the green bench, and out the schoolyard opening. Alan was stepping down from the concrete sidewalk to cross the asphalt street. Donny grabbed him and kicked the brief case from his hand. It fell and wobbled on the concrete curb, before dropping to the pavement. Grasping the shocked boy's jacket, he screamed, "Hey, you mother fucker! You called me a moron."

Before Donny's first punch landed on his face, Alan responded, "What? I don't even know you!" The boys on opposite sides of the field merged into a funnel to get out of the gate. Girls got off the bench to follow. Sarah yelled, "What the hell are you doing, Donny?" A circle formed around the two boys. A chorus of "Kick his ass" rang out. Donny's skinny fist hit the innocent victim. Alan made feeble moves to protect his face. Fat Peachy flicked his wrist down, pointed to Alan, and said, "Leave him alone, Donny. He's a faggot."

The worn waistband of the pack felt like the stiff curb against my neck and woke me. Even with cloud cover, I was hot. I glanced past my boots at the acacia. The shadow near its base confirmed that it was midday. I had barely lifted my neck from the black waistband, and the fly already was above me, like the private helicopter of a tiny couple, waiting for instructions. Past him, the western wall had taken on a copper color. I glimpsed the target weeds. There was nothing I could do to them in daytime. I pushed back along my familiar track to escape the light. It was cooler than Sunday and Monday, but the weight of hot air against my chest was oppressive. My faithful companion settled down near the pocket of my dirty white shirt. I closed my lids.

I stood horrified in the middle of the pack of tough guys. Donny refused to listen. He relished the egging on. Alan moved his hands to protect himself as Donny pushed him onto the sidewalk and along the mesh fence. The mob followed. Pushing to the front, I said, "That's enough, Donny." I reached out and grabbed his shoulder. He backed off. Alan picked up his scuffed briefcase and turned to the trestle for the train to Manhattan. With his head held high, Donny led the mob toward the fence. Shouts of "Way to go" filled the air. Everyone entered the park. The girls sat down on the bench. The teams lined up on opposite ends of the schoolyard, as if nothing had happened, and I lifted my leg for the kickoff.

The sun in my face woke me. I pushed my back up against the wall. I must have slept well, because the acacia's shadow had turned completely away from its base, exposing the entire burnt trunk. The shadow of the plant made a black stripe across the sands and onto the flat rock. I saw the afternoon was moving on 4 p.m. It was still hot on the grey sand, but the sleep in the reduced temps had raised my energy. I rubbed my hands on my thighs. My legs were stronger. I glanced from the shadowed rock to my life saving weeds. Again, I measured the distance. I had to get there. A vision of red flames.

Out of the corner of my right eye, I saw a rainbow appear in the sky. The cobalt blue and rose dome hung like a soft stadium light over the lip of the cliff above my right shoulder. It made me want to see the basin. Except for staring at the sky and the strange town lights in the distance at evening, I hadn't looked outside of Salvation Canyon since I arrived. I grabbed my stick in one hand and held the wall with the other as I lifted myself off the canyon floor.

I limped a few feet from the wall closer to the opening where I had slipped in. I scanned the basin. The mystery of the desert and the magic memories of glowing cholla returned for a few seconds, then left. The cracked land was dotted with tawny grasses. Everywhere were lonely rocky outcrops. To the south and east, large hills limited the extended plains. The rainbow's glow lit a patch of cumulus clouds above a series of mountain ranges descending to the horizon. It was hard to stand up and look for more than a minute. Someone had to reach me through the fissured hills and cracks of Joshua Tree; I sure couldn't reach them.

I sat in the sand and eyed the weeds, then unzipped the bottom sack attached to the pack and grabbed the emergency kit. The last fire starter was lying in a crease at the bottom. I pulled out the six-inch piece of compressed wood and clutched it like the lifesaver it might be. It looked like part of a primitive life raft. I gazed at the northern wall, saw two spots where pieces could be placed beneath the weeds, and broke the starter in half. I crouched down like a handicapped sprinter at the start bell. With the pieces and matches in my left hand and the stick grasped by the right, I limped towards the plants.

I was zapped. I leaned on my stick and watched my legs creep alongside. I had to stop and sit at the rock because my breath was heavy after only fifteen yards. I could not remember, sitting and waiting for dark with the fly, that guy who had jumped down a rocky ravine or the me who had marched across a basin enchanted by glowing cholla. The pool of resin by the acacia, fifteen yards back, looked like a far-off oasis with a deep pond. My own tracks by the southern wall seemed miles and years away — the marks of a distant caravan.

The fly and I waited while the moon brightened and increased in size, then my companion and I lifted off the flat rock, and I stuck the stick into the sand. I limped across the chalky ground with the fly a foot above my shoulders. Traveling at five feet per minute, we passed a patch of busted white blocks that looked like God once threw a concrete curb from the projects onto the floor of the canyon. I reached my target. The sharp features of the canyon merged, and the weeds blended with the water cracks in the wall behind them. The sturdy survivors didn't look so defiant in the soft twilight.

I stuck the fire starters in two spots in the phalanx of weeds and clump grass. In the dusk, I turned my head back to look at the sad blackened acacia that I'd tried to burn.

It was also a moonlit night, but the moon hung on the project fences. The kids were on the benches near the entrance. Donny and Patty had insulted some tough Puerto Rican guys from the Bronx. The guys from the Bronx knew we lived near the 67th Street train stop. Everyone listened for the sound of the train from the city. Peachy said, "Troy better get here soon." For a minute, the sound of a train drowned out the murmurs of the surf and then, ten muscular boys we didn't recognize walked down off the trestle. They entered the park and sat on a diagonal from us.

Troy walked in from the 56th Street side with two companions. All three walked at a very slow pace. Troy all in black, as usual; black skin, a black fedora, black jeans, and a black t-shirt. His bony arms hung loose from the shirt. He had a slim silver chain around his neck. A very muscular mulatto with iron knuckles on one hand accompanied him. A frail, short, older man walked in the middle. The man wore an eye patch and had a purple and lime doo rag on his head.

The Puerto Ricans got off the bench. The tallest two strolled out to meet our trio. Troy jitterbugged in front of the strangers, raised his bony right hand, turned back, and pointed to the man in the doo rag, "This here is Salem, warlord of the Hamels Projects." Troy stepped back. The frail Salem walked out. The moon shone on his pockmarked face. The kids on the benches whispered.

I crouched like a coyote with his snout stuck into the weeds; it was impossible to light the glossy tip of the match. But, practically a PhD with those God-damned matches by then, I straightened my legs and struck from above. The match caught fire. I placed it under a starter and waited. The flames flickered but failed to grow. The calm of the canyon disturbed me. I'd never get out. Befuddled and desperate, I crawled a few feet over to light my last piece of fuel.

I crouched beneath the grasses on my knees and propped the starter up on a small rock to give it more air. The match lit on my first try. This time the grasses above the starter caught and red flames engulfed the surrounding vegetation. I was thrilled to see fire spread from weed to weed as flames from the tops of the lit grasses engulfed their immediate neighbors. I crawled back and watched the entire pha- lanx become a horizontal red band, leaping along the western perimeter of Salvation Canyon. The sound of hissing flames filled the cavern. Black smoke rose from the fire to the top of the cliff making a ribbon of black and red.

Even the moon was eclipsed by the smoke. But soon the tops of the flames fell down the cliff and licked the blackened canyon bottom as the magnificent conflagration fizzled out. I hoped with all my might that my final fire had attracted attention from that community in the west. The fly and I sat and waited on the flat rock. A half hour after the fire fell, those lights went on across the desert, as they had every night before. We waited for a sound of searchers in the brush, or the sign of a flashlight, but nobody crossed over to us.

By my count, I was pretty sure I'd been lost five days. I was sure somebody must be looking for me. I turned my eyes from the red lights of the village and looked up in the sky, figuring that one of the helicopters I had seen days earlier was near my canyon now. The pilot had seen the flames from the air, and he would soon swoop down to get me, I'd be lifted up in his helicopter and taken to my car, and Salvation Canyon would be only a memory. As I visualized my rescue, my pulse quickened, but a dull hour after the fire died, my hope turned to ashes. Nothing was happening. I felt as used up as my kindling. I hobbled back to the acacia and dragged my pack to my scratched-over patch at the south wall. With the waistband of my pack beneath my neck, I looked at the moon, my companion for days. I had not just gotten to know her. She always arrived when needed.

The moon waited outside the bookstore on 5th and Main and lit the storefront. Teka Lark, the poet-activist, leaned over the counter and told the manager, "We're here from the Poet Walk." The manager waved her ahead. A few people sitting in chairs stopped perusing. They put their books in their laps. The room filled with voices not heard by day. Richard McDowell, dressed in his prison stripes, read to the surprised audience from his book *Homeless on Spring Street*. I introduced myself. "I'm the Poet Broker. This is my anthem for the Eastern Columbia Building." I began to read.

Don Garza took a video of the reading. Except for a few customers that walked in and out in front of Don's camera, the room was mellow. We got a good hand from the crowd. Afterward, Teka Lark said, "Hey, hold on. A lady from the *LA Times* is coming to meet us." We waited on the sidewalk in front of the window display. The reporter came down Main Street with a pad in her hand and greeted the street poet. "Hi Teka, sorry I'm late." By the time the interview ended, the moon had moved north to the black dome of the Hellman Building. Teka and I walked down 5th Street, and I smoked a joint.

The empty sand looked like an empty beach where forceful people like Teka Lark landed. I never thought to call the *LA Times* for coverage of the Poet Walk. I took a last look at the lonely canyon and closed my eyes. Instead of a squad of rescuers coming over the canyon walls, a squad of tiny sand flies swarmed from the ground and tickled my lips. I covered my mouth and pushed myself against my pack. With my body and makeshift pillow moved a few feet, the tiny creatures rose to follow in a large insect cloud and covered my torso.

I'm not sure if the fire had alerted an entire colony to my presence or if their restlessness was a coincidence, but wherever the horsefly and I moved in our sandy impression along the wall, the tiny flies popped from the sand and hovered around my head. I covered my face with my hat, but the troupe snuck through a bend in the rim. The moon shone on the flat large rock in the middle of the canyon. It was anchored at the center, but its edges were six inches above the ground. The space might keep the army of tormentors away. I left my pack along the wall, limped by the acacia, and reached the rock. The sand flies didn't follow us. Guided by lit lines of silica, I searched for a level spot on the flat rock to place my head, then lay on my back and pulled my hat behind my head for a cushion. The loyal horsefly settled on my chest.

In a shiny dark, cubicle-sized room whose walls, floors, and ceilings were black, I was the only sentient being, lying on my back on a bed which was not visible. Nothing moved. Something outside the boundaries of the room gave off a red light. Suddenly I heard my mother-in-law, Minnie Kaplan, screaming, "Where are you, Eddie?" I pushed down on my hands to lift my torso and found myself on the rock in the middle of the canyon, my stick beside me.

The sky was disorienting. Vega and the Northern Cross had moved on, but Orion wasn't yet up, puffs of clouds floated past unfamiliar constellations in a milky mix. Seeing my pack at the foot of a cliff wall lit by the moon, I leaned on the stick, got off the rock, limped to my pack, and pulled it alongside the scarred acacia. The horsefly was already next to me. The sand flies were gone! I turned the pack to face Orion in the morning and went back to sleep.

IX.

By TUESDAY NIGHT, Ranger Dan Messaros had already completed calls to associates and checked out the motel room in Desert Hot Springs, finding no new clues. Morongo volunteers had found no new prints. None of the search and rescue groups had anything to report. Four days after "the victim" had left for his hike there was the danger of severe dehydration. The helicopter and search teams had been looking for him near Warren View but had found nothing.

Joling decided to form his own team to see if he could get more concrete leads. "It was me, Deputy Mary Lou Brown, and SAR volunteer Tom Humphreville," he later told an investigator. His intent was to find out where Mr. Rosenthal had left the trail and to move the search area there. "Tracks are physical evidence. They lead searchers to a place where there is a greater probability of finding the missing person."

Joling and his team loaded up on water and went back to where the abandoned car was first found. Knowing the scene had been contaminated — a lot of people had walked over the tracks — the sheriff took new photos and measurements of shoe tracks at the driver's side door. He found out that there was one set of tracks, leading right from the driver's door, that stood out from any others in the area. "Everybody has a distinctive wear pattern," he explained later. "And Mr. Rosenthal's shoe had an extra lug that none of the others in the area had."

Sheriff Joling printed up copies of the new footprints and gave them to all the search and rescue teams, telling them, "We're going to Warren Loop. If we can figure out where he went off the trail, we'll notify you."

Carrying the new copies of the prints, the three trackers saw matching footprints go across the soft sand in a wide part of a wash and back on the narrow, hard-packed part of the trail. The intuitive sheriff realized, "The hiker thought he was on the wrong trail, so he didn't go back down the mountain. He had to go off. He went above the trail, found an easy place to walk, then his tracks disappeared — we knew he must have jumped."

At this point, Joling and his team made a decision that changed the direction of the search. "Here's what really happened," he said. "We saw he walked off the trail and went into a narrow channel. That's where he jumped down. From there, he was funneled into a deep ravine, leading to a series of drop-offs that got bigger and bigger. I saw that he started off with a good stride. Judging by the distance between his steps, he had good energy. I made a decision to keep going. And go we did. We did it the old-fashioned way — step by step. We went after him the whole night."

Day six
Wednesday, September 29

Wednesday morning Joling and his team climbed to the top of a hill. With the little battery power they had left on their cell phones, they called in their coordinates and asked the team to drop in searchers. They were at Little Long Canyon, where the terrain goes from ravine systems to canyons. They were dehydrated. The helicopter dropped water and ground troops. They took Mary Lee Brown back. She was exhausted and extremely dehydrated.

They looked around the area. It opened into a small valley, three hundred by six hundred yards. They decided Mr. Rosenthal did not go past there — they checked beyond that point. No tracks. "We got to something we didn't expect — complete cloud cover, and white sand. You couldn't see anything."

I woke up Wednesday in the same location but with a changed situation. The atmosphere felt and looked different. Orion was missing in action. His nursery of baby stars, gone. The moon shone limply through a gray overcast sky. The air against my sleeveless arms was cool. Best of all, a line of cumulus clouds took on a pink cast. I remembered the old sailor's rhyme, "Red sky at night, sailor's delight. Red sky at morn, sailor be warned." Hope rose inside me, hope that it would rain. I had forgotten what thirst was when the itchy feeling in my throat had left days earlier. But as I prepared for my morning tasks in Salvation Canyon, with the promise of rain under the encouraging sky, my body remembered deep inside.

Ready for my skin-moisturizing ritual, the fly lifted off my chest, but I couldn't sit up. My spine had melted away. I could not support myself. My torso fell forward onto my knees, and a shock registered throughout my being. I leaned on my hands and brought my upper body vertical, leaned on one hand to grab my pack with the other, and put it on my knees. I propelled my body backward by pushing my hands against the sand on both sides of my butt, and in a few minutes, reached the cliff fifteen feet away. My butt crammed against the wall to support my spine; I sat up.

Attached to ritual, I opened the last of the cream and dabbed the dried scabs on my arms. I bent forward to soothe my legs then was unable to lift my torso back against the wall without pushing my hands on the sand. Against the wall, with the fly on my knee, my torso fell forward, almost striking him. My spine didn't work. It didn't work. I had to lie down.

Unable to tell myself that I was dying, I took off my hat and leaned on my elbow long enough to write, "Wednesday — still here."

The wall was useless. I needed the spiritual support of my beloved acacia, a living breathing creature, and my base in the place. With the fly perched on my shoulder, at what felt like 10 a.m., I leaned forward and crawled hand over hand, dragging my legs behind me, to the patch of ground by the black and red trunk of the plant we had slept alongside since sheltering in the canyon. Turning my head as I lay down, I saw that my handprints lined the burrows my torso had made on my daytime odysseys to escape the sun's rays.

My boots stood a few feet from the acacia, where I had left them three days earlier. My unemployed knife and headlamp were stuck in the sand alongside the encrusted boots. On my hands and knees, I poured the remaining articles from my pack and placed everything around me in a circle, as if forming a compass on the sand. Making my boots North, the knife and lights were East and West respectively, and all other hiking essentials various points on the circumference. I had a sense of being watched from above, as if I was spider hanging from someone's thread.

All my hiking paraphernalia was around me. At my feet, the withered toilet paper, and between that and the knife, my unused compass. Between the headlamp and shoes, I placed the dead cell phone. There was a spot for the empty nylon medical pouch. I grabbed the trusty stick in my right hand and pulled it alongside me as I plopped down inside this ring. Having my belongings spread out around me made me feel secure. They both protected and represented me. They absorbed my plight. How important each useless article had become. I understood then one of the habits of the homeless, who employ shopping carts and plastic bags to keep their possessions alongside them always.

I thought of my wife Nicole sitting at her makeup table, fiddling around with her hair, lifting her makeup brush, wondering whether I'd return. One evening, we were driving through Beverly Hills. A homeless woman lay on a bus stop bench. Her bags bubbled up on both sides of her. My wife said, "These poor women, this is horrible." As the light changed, the woman sat up and took a can of dog food out from one of the plastic bags. A little dog popped out of her lap. I checked on the fly and closed my eyes inside my circle of belongings.

I stared down from thirty feet above the concrete corner of 4th and Main Street in Downtown Los Angeles. No longer in the Mojave Desert, my mind had crossed through the windmills of the San Andreas Pass and over the green San Bernardino Mountains. I looked at a dull scene below. All colors were muted gray and black. All the figures but one had hazy outlines. A homeless man in a tattered jacket pushed a shopping cart without bags. A blanket spread over the back of the cart, the metal bottom bars and the black rubber wheels showed through its empty frame. He pushed it off the curb in the face of cars riding the black pavement. The traffic slowed to allow him to cross, but he didn't.

Outlines of onlookers in colorless short sleeves walked behind him on the sidewalk. The deco carvings of the Hellman Buildings bent forward, bearing witness. The onlookers on the sidewalk, detachment on their faces, watched as the homeless man pushed his cart into traffic. I could not hear the horns honking below, but I could see drivers' hands bashing the steering wheels, see the angry faces. The short-sleeved workers shrugged. The man maneuvered his cart around the moving cars and turned left on Spring Street.

I opened my eyes. I was in my spineless situation under an undecided sky. The fly buzzed off my chest and circled my ring of possessions like a security guard on his rounds. I followed his flight, without lifting my body. From the corner of my eyes, I saw something extraordinary by the dull copper cliffs of the northern wall, thirty yards from last night's signal fire. Propped on my elbow, I turned my body toward the place. It was a spot where I'd never slept or walked. Rocks were rising from the grey selvage at the foot of the cliff wall. Hope rose in my chest. I had to reach the rocks.

I lifted my stick in my right hand, stuck it in the ground and leaned on it to raise myself to my knees, placed my free left palm on the ground, then jammed the stick into the ground ahead of me, lifted my torso a bit upward and forward, brought my knees beneath my midsection, took a breath and rested my knees on the sand. By doing this over and over, in a staccato motion of stick, knees, palm, torso, knees, I crawled by the acacia and left the circle of possessions. The horsefly rode on my shoulder beneath the cloudy sky.

We crossed the burrows and lines that my body and stick had left in the sand on my sleepwalking slides from the acacia to the southern wall. I felt no bigger than one insect carrying another. A cloud lifted and turned the rocks of Salvation Canyon russet. I lifted my head, placed my palms across the burrows and dragged my legs along. We got to the cliffs. We were on a threshold of smooth sand and stared up at a rock alcove that seemed to be growing as my perception of it sharpened.

First, the alcove grew a base that emerged from the craggy rocks of the cliff. As it expanded the niche, it took on a faint yellow color, and then lifted a few feet above the floor of the canyon. The walls it grew were smooth. It occupied a space apart from the northern cliff that it pushed back. Light glowed inside the pale-yellow space of the alcove. And that light, which was not anywhere else in the canyon, distinguished the niche from the rest of the rocks, as much as the fact that it was growing right in front of us.

I leaned on my elbows and stared. A fully-formed, fifteen-foot-high figure appeared. At the moment he materialized in his alcove, I was sure he came from the cliffs behind him, but I didn't see him come in. Unlike the alcove itself, he showed all at once. It was as if there was a portal that allowed him to enter from another dimension. His sudden appearance and calm demeanor suggested a messenger. My companion and I stayed on the desert floor looking up. The rim of the alcove glowed around his plain white hood. He was male. He did not speak. His bearing was that of a nobleman or royalty, but he wore an ancient tunic. A humble being unmindful of station. On my palms buried in the white sands, I was about five feet below him. The fly stuck to my shoulder as I crawled towards the visitor. His eyes desired to help me, to assist me. His pleated skirt was well pressed and held close to his slim waist by a simple leather belt. He emanated peace. Speaking the first words I had spoken in six days, I asked him, "What should I do?" I waited for something, and the desert responded. A ray of light lit his face. The sky turned blue.

The cliffs turned rusty copper as their metal shone. The sky darkened and stirred, and my question disappeared in the brewing sky as drops of precious water fell. The earth dimpled with brown pools. I took off my hat and felt water stream down my face into my mouth and swallowed the first drops of water in five days. The white sands dimpled with brown spots. But the drizzle stopped as quickly as it had begun. The holy messenger evaporated as the blessings of the rain ended. His canyon alcove became a vacant rupture in the rocky cliffs.

His was an energy I had felt twenty years earlier, when driving a rental car over a huge hill on the 10 Freeway to San Bernardino. I was in the extreme left lane when my engine shut down. My car rolled to a stop. Honking cars piled up behind me. Drivers cut around to my right as the traffic pattern shifted to fewer lanes. Some yelled curses from open windows. With traffic streaming by, there was no way I could get the car across six lanes to the emergency lane on the right side of the road. But suddenly traffic slowed in the lane to my immediate right.

A stranger appeared in my right side mirror. Like the canyon messenger, he popped from the ether. But unlike the messenger, he arrived on a vehicle. The canyon visitor had simple garb, but the motorcyclist was dressed head to toe in metallic silver. His motorcycle radiated light. Only the bottoms of his black tires were visible, since these were hidden by long silver fenders. The body of his bike — even the spokes of its wheels — was silver. As he stuck out his right hand to stop the astounded drivers in the lane to our right, I noticed a silver cross on his polished helmet.

He pulled up next to my car and lifted his visor. It stopped at the cross. With his right hand held behind him to hold back traffic, he motioned with his left for me to get out and push my car over into the lane to our right. When I did so, he held his hand out to slow traffic in that lane. Grateful cars sped by on our left. He moved to the next lane and held back cars and repeated the process as I moved safely across the six-lane freeway. Once I was in the security of the extreme right-side of the road, he left without saying a word. I stood up and watched him drive off. I saw his back fender had a cross and the word "Jesus" inscribed on the surface. When he dropped from view, I told myself, "This California is fucking unbelievable, just fucking unbelievable."

It was obvious to me that the visitor to the canyon wasn't Jewish, but I'm a Jew. Uncomfortable with his reappearance in my life, I turned my torso to crawl back to the familiar acacia. For me, a Jew in the desert, she was my base, my ground, my roots. On cue, the fly, who had been buzzing over the water drops, jumped on my shoulder as a powerful push propelled me on hands and knees, like a reversed magnet, to my spot by the bush. I crawled on the ground without once looking back to The Visitor, this Christ-like figure.

We were Yom Kippur Jews, if that. Not devout. But when I was in second grade, rushing to play after school, my brother sat me down on a green project bench. I could tell he had bad news. He put his left arm on the highest slat, around my shoulder, and said, "You know, we have to start Hebrew School this year."

"What, another school? When do we have to go there?"

"Today." He smiled as he answered.

We walked up the long dark stairway inside the Downtown Talmud Torah and crossed a narrow landing to a large, poorly lit room with tall walls. A bunch of old men in short sleeves, with grey beards and black yarmulkes, sat at a long wooden table near the rear. A small, bent guy got up and motioned for me to approach the table. I smelled his whiskey breath ten feet away. I sat down next to him. He stuck a Hebrew book in front of me with his bony arms protruding from his stained white shirt. He had a gentle but far-away stare in his eyes. He pointed to the black letters and began to pronounce these. I ducked his bad breath as best I could.

My parents let me drop Hebrew school for a few years, but a Jewish boy has to get ready for his Bar Mitzvah. I ditched a lot, snuck to the soda fountain daily with my friend Stanley, until a slap across my face from Dad for my blank report card got me quickly back to Hebrew School. But I never learned to read or comprehend the strange letters.

When my thirteenth birthday approached, I began Haftorah lessons. As the tutor searched his black book for my piece, I prayed for a tiny section, but he pointed to a forty-six-line selection and said, "This is yours." He never told me it was the prophet Ezekiel or translated the curses he was placing on the Jews for not following God. He pointed to each word and pro-nounced it, nudging me to mimic him, but the sounds fled my mind before I reached the bus stop. I sat on the bus and stared at the silent pages.

I memorized every first word in each of the forty-six lines and let that word trigger the sounds to come, so that line by line, I fought to the finish. It didn't matter if I recognized a single letter; I made the sounds.

On my big day, I dressed in my new suit; my Mom smoothed my hair back and "qvelled" over how nice I looked, beaming at me with pleasure. My parents drove me to the synagogue. The rabbi left me alone on the bimah, in front of the entire congregation. After I read two lines, I seemed to be lifted up, seeing myself and the congregants in their pews below. While I was suspended above the bimah, hearing Hebrew pour from my mouth and viewing worshipers below, I watched scores of ancient Jewish adults and children, in a variety of robes and rough clothing, move across the high windows of the temple.

At the blackened trunk of my wounded plant, the sky was a bland off-white. The pink tinges on low-lying clouds were gone. The walls had lost their rust luster and had returned to a dull brown. I patched together a prayer for rain around the Hebrew word, "adamah," or "earth," all I could come up with after decades of new age Judaism and a year of Hebrew with Rabbi Moshe downtown.

I knelt below the singed leaves and uttered my hybrid prayer to the Hebrew God, the blessing on vegetables:

Baruch atah A-donay, Elo-heinu Melech Ha'Olam borei pri ha-adamah.

The sky churned. Drops fell on my shoulders. The ground took on a softer shade of gray as water plinked onto the surface. I lay down with my stick alongside me and the headlamp at my feet. The drizzle glistened the cliffs. The wet walls seemed cozy and closer. It felt like God had built a shower for Ed Rosenthal in

Salvation Canyon. With my mouth wide open, I felt for each drop that hit my tongue and stretched my arms out with my palms extended as if my arms could drink. I felt blessed.

The drizzle turned to droplets and stopped after about five minutes, but the sky lightened only a little. Hoping for more rain, I fell asleep inside my personal circle of knife, tape, stick, headlamp, and moldering toilet paper.

Wednesday, Zoraster called an experienced military buddy of his, who told him, "They're probably looking for a body at this stage. But they won't tell the family that." Every day since Monday, Nicole and Hilary had driven from the Joshua Tree Best Western to the campground. They stood outside the circle of teams and saw the head ranger post the map results on the coordinating board at the daily briefing. But they heard no news until Wednesday morning when Nicole overheard Judy Barza say, "We think we know where he is."

"But is he alive?" Nicole asked into silence.

Inside my circle, as raindrops fell from the darkened sky, my eyelids would not stay open very long. The rain stopped. I slept. A light rain woke me. My tracks along the wall were muddied; my boots had tiny pools of water dotting the laces. I looked for my companion.

He was on my chest. My eyes shut. A breeze blew across my face.

The day moved on. My eyelids opened to a sound of a raindrop, a smell of damp grass in the basin, each change in light. But I was a disinterested witness. My mind was nowhere. Nothing registered. My lids closed quickly after each short opening. Hours seemed to pass in seconds. I noticed the light. The canyon walls flicked like a deck of cards.

Lying on the moist sands alongside my trusty stick, with the blessed breeze crossing my face, inside my circle of possessions, I was an ancient being about to travel to the next world. I turned my neck and opened my eyes for what I was sure was the last time and saw medieval warriors, in short skirts and tunics under chain link armor, inspecting the crags and cliffs. I heard them grunt and nod as they mounted the northern wall, and they saw what I could not — the broad sand basin of the Mojave decked out in Joshua trees, yellow bunchgrass, and the radient cholla, stretching as far as Palm Springs; they smiled broadly. I fell asleep certain they would be proud to die in Salvation Canyon.

Joling and Tom Humpreyville had left the search in others' hands on Wednesday morning. Exhausted from the long effort all night Tuesday, Joling slept. Waking late Wednesday afternoon, Joling contacted the searchers to see what was happening and was informed that Mr. Rosenthal had not been found.

X.

Day seven
Thursday, September 30

ON ALL PREVIOUS days on the Mojave, I woke before the desert lit. Thursday morning, I didn't wake of my own accord and wouldn't have woken at all, but late in the morning, I heard a sound. It disturbed me from the deepest sleep. I was dazed and couldn't make out my own location in the canyon. I was face down and propped myself up on my right elbow, straining my ears toward the source. It was outside the canyon past the northern wall. I saw the wall, but I couldn't see anything else. Without the strength to stay up or energy to lift myself, I lay down again, and seeing my possessions in the sand, remembered where my body was. My chin stayed propped up on the sand, my eyes directed at the sound.

A black metal object came into view. It hovered a hundred feet in the air, about fifty yards past the wall. A real live helicopter was outside Salvation Canyon. All the other copters I'd seen, or thought I'd seen, in Baby Canyon long ago, had no relation to me. They were just red and blue lights in a distant sky. But this one was so close I was able to make out the finish and color. Real metal, I remember saying to myself. A new element had come into being, not only in my life, but in the universe. The smooth black runners of the copter broke into the air and rocks, as if from an alternate dimension. The cliffs, the ground, and the atmosphere of Salvation Canyon were all of the source I was settling into, that I was about to become a part of. This piece of formed hardness was not. The intense physicality of the thing amazed me. A solid object floating in air, and so near.

The thing disappeared momentarily and then popped up, over the lip of the supernatural northern wall. I squirmed around on my stomach, trying to raise my arms, and noticed my friend the horsefly was gone. The air stirred wildly, and I heard a sentence boom, "Are you that Rosenthal that's out here?"

When I remembered that question afterwards, it seemed intensely funny, as if I would answer, "No, I'm not," or, "No, he's in the next canyon." But it was not funny at all. I screamed out to the best of my ability,

"Yes, I am!"

"Can you stand up?" asked the voice.

"Yes, I can," I answered.

I started to pull myself to my feet. I fell over, landing on my side. Seeing my condition, the pilot, whose face and headset were now clear, told me over the speakers, "We're coming around to get you."

The copter turned and merged with the sky. I watched it carry my rescuers out to the great basin. They were gone. The silence of the canyon was menacing as the thought that they might not return scared me. It took so very long, but soon I heard vibrations closing in on the canyon. They had turned and headed my way. I told myself that the pilot was looking for a place to land. The sound lit up my insides. I told myself, "I am going to survive." My heart filled with joy. I would leave this wonderful canyon alive. Nobody would have to find my hat.

Thoughts appeared in my mind. "Wow! I am tough!" and "What a survivor I am!" But my guts rejected those thoughts, which evaporated in two seconds. A different current overwhelmed me. Lying prostate on the sands, I filled with appreciation for the ramshackle cliffs that had hidden me from the brutal sun for days. I remembered how I first got to the magical ring of walls and felt thankful for the clamshell rock right outside which had hidden me in its black shadows on Sunday. My eyes turned to the graceful acacia. I had collapsed in her shade. I looked wistfully at the half green and half black trunk, and thanked the plant for its forbearance.

Waves of gratitude swept over me in remembrance of all the forces I owed my life to. The moon in the morning sky watched my rescue. She'd had been a compass on my shoulder in the journey across the cholla-dotted basin. Every night she had lit the sky like a light in a baby's bedroom. The giant Orion who woke my mornings like a red-eyed nurse. The Northern Cross — the sailor's compass — Blue Deneb — the sapphire of the sky — a beacon and a cradle toy.

The singular evergreen of Tree Canyon came to my mind. How I felt as if its branches pulled me up from the rutted road to hold me in its soft tufts. How it drew me deeper and deeper into its bough. I could not have survived the blistering sun of that horrible, glistening hillside.

I scanned my arms and legs for my friend. He had to be close to me if he was anywhere in the sunny canyon. From our moment entering this pile of rocks when he tacked himself to my shoulder, until I fell asleep in yesterday's flashing sequence of skies, he was within ten inches of me, hovering above my left arm every morning, and following me around the canyon. The copter closed in on the northern wall, hovering like him.

Above the engine vibration, I heard the delicious words, "We're coming in to get you." The branches of the acacia stirred as the copter landed on the sand. It rocked for a few seconds on its metal rails and straightened. A brawny brown-skinned man opened the cockpit and stepped down. My own Orion from the sky! He walked to me and scooped me out of the sand. He carried me in his arms, placed me in the rear seat of the waiting craft, and told me gently, "I'm going back to gather your things." His tall, silent companion turned to me and handed me a bottle of water. "Sip it slowly," he said. I opened it eagerly, poured the waterfall of blessings into my throat. It went down easily. But the water spewed out of me and all over the back of the pilot's seat and the floor. Smiling sheepishly, I made a motion to wipe things up with the tails of my filthy shirt.

The pilot returned, putting my things next to me in the back of the bird. As we lifted up out of Salvation Canyon, I heard him call in to his station to announce, "We've got him!" We rose quickly into the late morning sky. I looked down as the cliffs shrunk and blended with the chalky basin. The white face of the moon was small below us, hanging over the landscape like a lost balloon — not the large light leading me, not the beaming face of canyon evenings. I looked down at the beige hills. As we lifted, their contours blurred, and the landscape was undecipherable, green and brown spots on an off-white field. I was a buried seed. Something tiny, dredged from something gigantic, a mathematical miracle.

After an initial shock at seeing large orange cubes,

I recognized buildings. We landed in a parking lot. The glass copter doors swung up. Hospital medical staff materialized, and I was grabbed, strapped on a gurney. I wanted the husky man and his co-pilot to stay with me, but I was wheeled away. A wide door-frame passed above me. I entered a large well-lit room.

A multitude of nurses in green coveralls swarmed around me like sand flies, poking my arms, looking in my mouth. One stood alongside the gurney and patted my chest. "We're so glad to see you! Your wife will be here soon." Another must have wrapped a blood pressure monitor around my left arm and read numbers that told her something about me. I started hearing my heartbeat and turned my head to watch it on the machine. The repeated pokes of one nurse, searching my shrunken veins for her IV, felt like the tiny hedgehog spines that had jabbed and jabbed me. I thought of them fondly. After several tries, he succeeded and stuck a needle into the dehydrated arm.

They could have done whatever they wanted, as far as I was concerned. Only two hours earlier I was as good as dead. The pilot had lifted me from my grave and brought me to them. I couldn't raise my head to see what they were doing, but I felt safe. A corsage of fluids rolled in above my head on the metal arm of a cart. I turned to see them attached to the line. The jade green and violet vessels were like the yucca kites that dotted the skies on that spring hike to Warren View with the young men.

I fell asleep. I felt my wife's gentle hand on my forehead, "Thank God you're okay." Her arms around my shoulders, a kiss on my forehead. "You really scared us." I remembered her gentle voice on the stairs. "You think a heat wave is a good time for a hike in the desert?" She was tired, looked harried.

"Where's Hilary?"

"She's on her way."

Standing at the head of my gurney, my wife draped her arms around my shoulders and collapsed on my chest. It felt good to have her lying there. I dozed.

I heard the sweetest voice issue from a nurse who had turned from her paperwork on the counter and addressed me. "We're going to take care of you here." At the sight of the gorgeous blond, I forgot that I was a sunburned relic that had just lost fifteen pounds. "Where is my wife?"

"I think she went to speak to the press. You created a big stir around here," she said with a wide smile.

I grinned. "Did I? So, they knew I was a Downtown Los Angeles real estate broker?"

She laughed. I laughed along with her without knowing why. I looked at her face. It resembled my mom's wedding picture, the one hanging on the wall of the stairway at home.

"Do you know where my daughter is?" I asked.

"No, but I'm sure she's on her way."

"Where is the pilot?"

The platinum blond was joined by a matronly woman carrying little drinks in red and blue bottles. The universe plotting to remind me how stupid I was to leave the red and blue water bottles in my car's trunk. She handed me one, adding in a friendly southern accent, "You'll need to keep replenishing your liquids."

"Thanks. I threw up the water in the helicopter."

I glanced through the aperture of a curtain splitting the room, at an elderly woman. A young, downcast female had joined her at the foot of the bed. They sat on chairs and stared at the patient I could not see through the curtain.

"Say, who's that?" I asked the friendly southerner who had given me the drinks.

"There are no private rooms in the ICU, and not everybody in here is as lucky as you."

By "lucky," I thought she meant scot-free. I did not understand how much I was impacted and for how long I would be. My skinny legs meant that my body had eaten itself to stay alive, and the inability to keep my eyes open meant that I was used up, that you don't drag yourself on your back in hundred-degree heat for several days and just pop up one hundred percent. It hadn't reached me that a person who enters a death sleep doesn't necessarily wake up with the same mind.

The nurse drew the curtain between my bed and the other patient and returned to my side. After reviewing my medical tape, and glancing at my monitor, she put a finger to her lips, lifted her eyelids, and sighed. Still not hip to the full picture of what it meant to be in the ICU, I half got it and whispered, "Gosh, that's terrible. You mean he's really sick?"

"Sorry to say so. Now, you sit back and have your drink. We have things to take care of out here." She pointed to a grey bump attached to a cord on my bed. "Just push this button if you need us." She left.

Trying to keep my half-opened eyes off the obscured body behind the curtain, I looked at the green walls and listened to the beeps of my monitor overhead. I lifted the tiny red bottle to my lips and sipped. It was delicious

The matronly woman was back. A technician came in behind her, rolling a device on a tray. They stood a few minutes at the shelf alongside the window and checked the machine and some paperwork. My stomach tightened. My head leaned back in suspicion. The nurse turned toward me. The sensitive woman must have noticed that I opened my eyes as I twisted my nose in a bit of a snarl, because she assured me, "He's here to do a routine check on your heart."

"Oh, why's that?"

"Your wife told us you had a heart attack and bypass surgery."

The nurse lifted my robe, and her companion rolled a lubricated device over my ribs. In yellow hospital light, the hairs on my chest looked like desert short grass. I sighed in gratitude that grass wouldn't grow over my decomposed chest in the canyon. My lids closed and opened as the machine rolled over my ribs and I didn't pay much attention.

Half asleep, I saw my brother Joe enter the room through the door the technician exited and walk past the foot of my bed. He sighed, "I'm so glad we had Amma do special prayers for you." Bursting with gratitude for his Indian guru, he leaned over the right side of my bed and hugged me.

I looked at my innocent brother's face. Noticing the circles under his eyes, I told him, "You look worse than I do."

"Your wife kept us busy checking on the rescue every hour. We stayed with her in the Best Western in Joshua Tree the last five days." He grinned.

"Why don't you get some sleep finally?"

"Good idea."

I kissed my brother goodbye, and he exited the door behind me.

Had distant human's prayers penetrated into the

canyon?

My bedside phone rang — the President of our Temple 'Makom Ohr Shalom.'

"Hey buddy, I can't tell you how pleased we are."

"Sure, Harold. Thanks so much."

I sat up and pulled my hospital blanket to my shoulder. The two women walked out from behind the closed curtain: the older one was crying, the younger one had her arms around her.

"I know you need to rest, but I just want to play this for you."

I heard a recording of the congregation singing "Mishabera," a song of blessings. Harold got back on and said, "That's how we got you back safe."

I saw the congregation choir, my lost self, the moon, Salvation Canyon, the fly, and the Visitor. We were a page in a large format graphic novel. The choir was separated from the Mojave by a massive, miles-high, unmapped, impenetrable, blue glob.

Who would have taken credit had I died?

Victory has a thousand fathers, but defeat is an orphan.

I closed my eyes. When they opened, it took me a few seconds to see that my daughter Hilary was sitting in front of me on a visitor's bench at the foot of the bed. I had not noticed this bench before, and it seemed to arrive with my dear daughter on it. Her knees were crossed. Her black hair was pushed back, held by a rubber band in a little pony tail. She had a white sweatshirt on. There was an orange blemish on her forehead. Breathing excitedly, she explained why she was hours late. "I drove all across the desert to Palm Springs, but when I got there, they said you were in a different hospital." My gratitude. She had her Dad's lousy sense of direction. She confided, "I told them you were alive because you hadn't walked me down the aisle yet. I knew I was right." I smiled at the "high fence girl," remembered her climbing a forty-foot fence when she was six years old. The little girl turned her head down at me on the bench and yelled, "I can keep going, Dad."

The nurses dimmed the lights. I fell asleep, blessed. A gentle voice woke me, "I'm going to have you sit up a bit." It was the night nurse, a freckle-faced redhead. She raised my bed and explained, "so I can use this stupid toothbrush on you."

"Sure."

She slid the bed tray over me. It had a toothbrush in an unopened cellophane package, toothpaste, and a small basin.

"These brushes they give us are so soft they're ridiculous," she said. "The hospital lawyers are worried about brushing a patient's teeth too hard. Like we'd hurt somebody's mouth. Open up now."

Ripping open the packaging to get to the small

tool, she put paste on the bristles and squished it in the little basin. The paste bubbled up to white foam. White paste spreading down the handle onto her fingers as she stuck the brush into my mouth. She hovered over me like the moon on the lip of Baby Canyon. "Isn't that something?" she asked, without expecting an answer. I grunted in assent.

The next morning a doctor huddled with my wife at the nurse's counter. He handed her a printout of some kind. From the corner of my eye, I noticed that Nicole folded it carefully, inserted it in a zippered compartment of her shoulder bag, and after turning towards my bed, had narrowed her eyes and nodded her head. I'd seen those eyes mix concern and righteous indignation before, never a positive sign, but I dismissed it when they approached and the doctor confirmed what I thought, saying, "There's no reason for you to stay here. We're discharging you this afternoon." My wife smiled and patted her hand on my chest. She walked back around my bed with the doctor to confer about something. He exited out the rear; the soft thuds of his steps joined other noises of the corridor.

Nicole returned to my side and smiled, "I'll be back in a few hours with your brother." The fluids had done their work; I felt the urge of my bowels. There were no nurses around. I sat up and dangled my legs over the side of my bed. The friendly southern nurse had placed a cane at the side of my bed. I grabbed it and used it to support myself, circled the foot of my bed to reach the exit door. The restroom was a few yards beyond. My first bowel movement in a week was a reminder of more than a normal body function. I passed the peanut butter sandwich I had eaten at the peak, enjoying my view of blue San Jacinto across Palm Desert, the vision of paradise before descending into hell.

Back in my bed, a tiny dot on the desert. I pulled my top sheet snug. The blond nurse returned and said, "We were very happy to have you with us." I looked over at the partition and saw it was wide open. "Did they move him to another room?"

"No, I'm afraid not. We were all so pleased how you recovered."

My eyes felt sadness for the wife and daughter of the dead patient, but the sadness was followed by a tangible vibration of gratitude in my chest. The nurse said goodbye. I realized she would not be returning, and I asked, "Can I say goodbye to the night nurse?"

"No, she's gone for now," and then she repeated, "We were all happy to have you with us."

I wasn't satisfied. I wanted to say goodbye to all the nurses personally. I felt that they were each my personal friends and I was their personal patient, as if I was each one's only patient. Like the pilot, my personal hero, who materialized from the universe and lifted me in his arms. Each of the nurses had a personal connection to my vulnerability, and each came to nurture me apart from any shift or a hospital schedule.

It would take me time to learn that life was not like my journey on the desert, where I was the single soul enchanted by Purple Canyon, where I was the only child of the evergreen tree which succored me in the heat. Where I was uniquely loved and watched over by the moon, The Northern Cross, Blue Deneb, and my friend the fly.

The curtain was open, and the bed to my right was empty. I thought of myself as fully recovered and was ready to get home. The room itself was ready to move on. It had things to do. It had had enough of Ed Rosenthal, and the only part of him that was left, was he himself. The walls were restless and rustled me out of bed.

I stood and examined the empty curtain tract in the ceiling to the right of my bed, checked the flat-head screws holding it in place and the tightness with which adjacent pieces had been aligned. I turned away from the track when I heard noises in the corridor, which I mistook for someone coming to get me.

I pulled my hospital gown over my head and put it on the bed. The t-shirt Nicole had brought swam on my shoulders. I sat facing the empty space to my right and positioned my jeans on the floor below my legs. I rubbed my burnt skinny legs to thank them and pulled my pants up to my knees. I stood and raised them to my waist. They started to slip off. I held them with one hand and inserted my belt in the pant loops with the other. I tightened the belt to a mark two holes tighter than before my disappearance.

Hospital carts rolled through the corridors of the ICU. Footsteps and greetings met in the hallway outside. I listened for a sound, as if I was to be rescued by the helicopter again but this time from a room in High Desert Medical Center where I had been placed only minutes after leaving those stone walls. I was still listening and waiting.

A green-suited man brought a collapsible wheelchair into the room. He opened it and coaxed me into the padded seat, put the bag of my belongings in my lap, and wheeled me down the corridor to the hospital exit. The door opened. My wife's car was parked on a strip of pavement surrounded by coarse beige sands with tight, yellowed grasses. A Joshua tree curled its high limbs twenty yards past the car's hood. My brother smiled at me from the driver's seat. Nicole settled in front in the passenger seat. "We're going to get your car," she said without turning around.

"Oh, right."

Joe picked up a road that ran along the desert out-skirts. I sat in the back and felt beguiled and repulsed as I gazed at the undulating hills and was sure I saw my worn-out-self trekking in the visible heat Friday and Saturday, jumping down hillsides and over deep cracks in the rock.

Bands of gravel circled campsites and cars at the Joshua Tree campground. There was yellow tape on the ground. A crime scene, and I knew the tape was for me. We waved goodbye to Joe. "We'll see you in L.A.," Nicole called to him. We walked along some oversize tire treads and crossed the tape around my car. The isolated vehicle looked alien to me. My wife took my bag. She popped the trunk.

A young man appeared, and though there was a line of trees about thirty yards back, it seemed he came out of the ground.

"Are you the lost hiker?"

"Yes, I am."

"Are those your boots in that bag?"

"Yes." He came closer. He smiled at Nicole then asked me, "Do you mind if I see one up close?"

"No, not at all." I pulled a boot from the bag and handed it to him. He turned it sole up and looked at the tread carefully, as if it were a fingerprint.

"Wow. That's amazing. This is it. I thought we'd never find you." He felt the nubs of the sole with his fingertips, then shook my hand and handed the boot back to me. "It's an honor to meet you," he said.

"Thanks so much." A current of thought bypassed my mind. My heart glowed. I placed the boot laces-down inside the bag, and in the few seconds before I closed the trunk, I saw the pattern of the treads imprinted in the desert sand and felt in a way I belonged there, would always be there. Nicole pushed the ignition button, and I was startled by the car's vibration. She backed out over the yellow tape, and we followed the gravel out of the campground parking lot.

At the exit, there was a flyer posted on a tree. "Missing hiker," it read. Above the lettering, I saw a picture of myself. But it was not a complete identification, only a partial one, and time would teach me that my feeling for the picture was a hint of the feelings I'd forever feel for my post-desert self, and my impression of myself, like my sense of other beings, the blessed pilot and the kind young rescuer, seemed to come from nowhere and quickly evaporate. At times I would experience myself as a pop-up, finding myself in the company of others, but not quite there, not certain how I came to be there, detached, belonging somewhere else, maybe in the last tread of my boot print.

Once we reached the Twenty-Nine Palms Highway,

other cars joined us, and reverberating together we made one sound, a single tribal energy vibrating through the permeable metal barriers of the vehicles, filling the air. Our car's side walls might as well not have been there. With my back against the rear seat, my eyes scanned side to side, watching the pack gain visible cohesion. The sounds resounded like signals from car to car. The swarm of buzzing cars descended the shale hills of Morongo Basin, past the coffee shop, and Nicole merged with the 10 Freeway. She accelerated. I leaned back and took a sip of water from my jug as our pack joined thousands of colored metal packets of energy heading towards the sun.

"This is absolutely unbelievable."

"What is?" She glanced in the rear-view mirror and changed lanes.

"Everything. Astounding."

She looked at me. Her eyelids lifted in response, and her head twisted a bit off axis. I returned her gaze, then lost contact when she watched a car cut across her windshield to exit. She looked back in the mirror. I watched her push her hair away from her face. She negotiated with the stream of cars off Highway 111 West merging with the traffic entering the San Gorgonio Pass out of the desert. Her eyes kept to the driver's side mirror as she joined the lanes lining up in the left for the long stretch to Los Angeles.

The ten-foot post seemed to rise at least a hundred feet to the ceiling. Our modest townhome seemed a palace, the milky skylight suspended sky-high. I walked up the steps, which seemed a far climb to the first landing, turned and went to the top, crossed along the small parapet to our bedroom, and looked down. The painting above the couch seemed immense and the wall a tower. I leaned over, from the surprising height of our landing, and looked down and out through the window to our garden of pink and yellow impatiens — it was a palace courtyard. Now I went to the bedroom, lay down, and heard the sounds of Nicole leaving. I was in a purple canyon, inside the high canopy of lavender stones. In the soft white sands, it was early afternoon, and the sun was high in the sky. A pink light with a yellow fringe grew in the space between my eyes and expanded like a screen inside my head as it eclipsed the view of the canyon. Tears seeped from my closed eyes.

Tears over a place that surprised me. Longing for the canyon, I saw myself stepping on rocks and around yellow grasses in the heat, walking in and out of the rock walls. I sat up, opened my eyes and walked across the landing to my office right off the landing.

My cell phone rang. It was my friend Jack. "Hey, I can set up a press conference at Clifton's Cafeteria for tomorrow. Is that too soon?"

"No, tomorrow is fine." I did not understand what he meant, by "too soon." I was fully engaged in believing I was fully engaged. But I hadn't come back from the desert, and I didn't really want to. I was on temporary assignment with my family, my work, and everything else. It is not the same as wanting to get away from my wife as always and wanting to be done with raising my daughter as I always did. And being sick of the clients and dreaming of getting away from them as everyone who knows me knows I always wanted to.

This is a different going away, because I never returned. And I'm playing the part of this guy who wants to get away and watching his dramas and schemes without really being him. That's why it's very easy to be in and out of the longing. And in one minute, I'm planning to disappear and in the next figuring out my wife's Mother's Day present. Just as before, but much more rapidly without as much internal drama. Or dropping then soliciting the same client in one day, while watching it all.

EPILOGUE

I WAS IN the kitchen enjoying my cereal when Nicole came down the steps. "Honey, don't forget your medical test for the cardiologist."

"Oh, didn't surviving the desert prove I was in shape?"

"Don't be silly. The doctor wants to be sure your heart is good."

I had to admit that it didn't sound bad. I told myself that I'd show that cardiologist. A few days later, I drove to Santa Monica. I parked on the street and rode up the elevator carrying a change of clothes. I was determined. The nurse on duty brought me into the room and checked my vitals. "I'll be right back," he told me.

He returned with a heart monitor that he strapped around my chest over my t-shirt, and pointed to the treadmill. "It will start slow and then speed up."

"Right, okay."

"The supervising physician will be right in."

The physician entered. His badge said Cardiologist. He explained, "You don't have to complete all the levels, only what you are comfortable with."

"That's fine," I answered, but I had something else on my mind.

I got on the machine, and the belt moved below me. It felt like nothing was happening. The thing started accelerating. As the rubber pad sped beneath my shoes, the doctor asked, "How do you feel?"

"I feel great." That was the truth. The treadmill landscape repeated itself. I passed the twisted Joshua tree, the gnarled guardian I first saw from a half mile below at the bottom of the sandy undulation. My feet left behind the dark, tiny creosote leaves and burnt yellow grasses of that hill and crossed over the crest. I was tired. I had no water. It was late. A Joshua tree held a weird angle beneath a band of red sky on the new ridge. I was sure I was near the top.

"Are you feeling okay? The test is excellent," said the cardiologist.

"Yes," I said through heavy breaths.

I reached the ridges. I jumped across the twelve-foot gap. It led to a steep descent. I couldn't stand up where the plants were thirty degrees to the blue sky. I tumbled over the large mound of dirt. If the burnt ocotillos lived, so would I.

I had to stand up. I had no choice. I kept going.

"We've done enough." I heard the doctor.

"No, let's finish it up! Be sure to make notes."

The doctor smiled and marked his chart. The treadmill raced. I felt and saw inside me the muscle, bones, and grimace of a rough man with a shadowy beard, pumping my legs, pounding the treadmill. A guy who would step on anything and anyone to survive.

"That's enough," said the doctor, and he moved a knob on the treadmill. The machine slowed and stopped. I got off as an attendant entered the room. He removed the device from my chest.

"You can change into your street clothes."

"Sure." I sat on a bench. As I changed from my shorts, my breathing settled. I took the elevator to street level and turned my attention to the flowering jacaranda trees.

The next day, I felt like checking out Downtown. I walked from my office to Pershing Square. The inside of the park was dotted with homeless people and their sleeping bags stretched across the raised concrete ribs throughout the park. The closer I got to Fifth Street, the more bedding I saw. I passed a shaded portion near the exit, which is popular with some of the street people and homeless. A black man, sitting on the ground, came into view. The slim gentleman in worn but clean shirt and trousers had a thin beard on his face. He leaned back and greeted me, "Hey, are you that broker that was lost in the desert?'

Astounded, I responded. "Yes, I am."

"I prayed for you," he said modestly.

"That's amazing. Thanks so much."

"Never mind that," he said, lifting one nostril and tilting his head. He went on, "Have you thought about who saved you?"

"No, I haven't."

"Well, you better."

The rocks of the canyon split open. A pedestal appeared. It was in a separate space. The fly and I looked up at a figure growing from the rocks. He was bent on helping anyone he found. The light was his. He came from nowhere.

Months later, I went back to Salvation Canyon with Ken and Wendy Sims of Sky Valley. We crawled under a water district fence and walked three miles. They took me to the side they knew, but it was the wrong side. I led them in a mile-long walk clear around the canyon. We made our way around the thirty-foot-high walls that had sheltered me for five days. Now, we turned right, and there it was, the clamshell rock. There was no mistaking the rough-faced feature where I had crouched and slept crumpled up, beaten down. We entered the opening through which I had escaped the heat. It was a holy place for me. Salvation Canyon. A large coyote squash had flowered in the gap between the rock walls, its rough yellow insides open in a tight half-eaten spool. The white ground flecked with grey had been filled by spring rains with green blades of short grass.

"You probably want some time alone with your canyon."

They were gone, and the silence that had filled my ears for five days returned. I strode over to my first friend, the graceful acacia. Fresh green limbs with small cat claw leaves stretched from its reddish trunk, and the black patches of its branches had almost healed in my absence. I moved to the southern wall. I looked for impressions left by my body when I could only slink or crawl, but the desert was swept clean.

There were still flecks of copper color in the wall, and I wanted to look behind me towards the green tipped weeds where the visitor had arrived, but a sense of dread, of impending death, came up from the canyon floor. A terror froze me where I stood, uncontrolled, vibrating. I tried to turn, but couldn't move. An un-realized threat. I shook with the fear I hadn't felt when I was stranded in the blinding heat of summer, drained, dehydrated, and near death.

I clutched at the cord around my neck, and I blew my emergency whistle.

ACKNOWLEDGMENTS

I'M INDEBTED TO my wife Nicole and daughter Hilary for inspiring the imaginary communication which prolonged my survival on the Mojave in 2010. But I could only last so long. Absent the steadfast efforts of The National Park Service, San Bernadino sheriffs, and volunteer Desert Search and Rescue teams, my family would never have seen me again. This book would not be.

I want to thank my friends of fifty years ago for filling Salvation Canyon with my memories. I changed the names of two teens who encountered tragedy in one of my passages.

I owe special thanks to volunteer Robert Mohler of the Morongo Basin Search and Rescue; without him, I'd never have known my own story. Thanks also to Palm Desert Search and Rescue for the final map and the introduction to an entire rescue team. Thank you to Ken and Wendy Sims, who photographed Salvation Canyon before the desert swept away the evidence of my sojourn and rescue.

Without the help and encouragement of so many, this memoir wouldn't see the light of a lamp. The book would not exist without L.A. novelist and teacher Susan Wyler. Her dogged persistence over the last three years carried me through. Writer and editor Anton Mueller of Culver City evaluated five different earlier drafts.

My thanks to Doppelhouse Press. I deeply appreciate publisher Carrie Paterson's belief in my writing and in the primacy of the writer's own voice. I'm so grateful that my poetry publisher Maja Trochimczyk of Moonrise Press also got behind this prose endeavor.

Thanks to writing coach Ina Hillebrand for helping with an early version of this memoir. I'm so very fortunate to have had surf/ punk artist and PR man, Jack Skelley, encourage my development as a writer.

Six years ago, my wife attended a conference in San Diego and came back with a signed copy of *Wild* by Cheryl Strayed. Nicole had shared my experience and my memoir struggles with her. The writer sent me a note: "To Ed. Continue moving forward."

Thanks, Cheryl. I did.

"POET-BROKER" ED ROSENTHAL has saved many Art Deco-era structures and businesses in Downtown Los Angeles, including The Eastern Columbia Building and Clifton's Cafeteria.

Rosenthal's socially-oriented poetry has been featured in the *Wall Street Journal*, the *LA Times*, and *Urban Land*, the national magazine of the Urban Land Institute. He is known for his poetry performances and his environmental poetry, which is found on Sierra Club sites and in California poetry journals.

As a survivor of a desert ordeal, Rosenthal has been featured in "Fight to Survive" on The Outdoor Channel, Bear Grylls' "Escape from Hell" series, the *Jewish Journal of Greater Los Angeles*, several presentations on The Weather Channel, *Los Angeles Magazine*, and "The Story" on National Public Radio.

He lives in Culver City with his wife, Nicole.